PASSION
FOR
POSSIBILITY

Moving Beyond
Believing
INTO
KNOWING

PASSION
FOR
POSSIBILITY

Moving Beyond
Believing
INTO
KNOWING

JOSE FELICIANO CFP®, ChFC, CLU, LUTCF

Exposition House Press
NEW YORK

Exposition House Press
244 5th Avenue, Suite 200
New York, N.Y. 10001
www.ExpositionHouse.com

Printed in the United States of America

First edition published 2009. Second edition published 2023 and, in part, contains previously published materials.

Photography credits: page 39, dreamstime.com; page 70, iStockphotos.com; page 85, Zubin Mehta by Marvin Hamlisch; page 97, Getty Images; page 140, iStockphotos.com; page 144, dreamstime.com; 149, Public Domain. All other photographs are from the author's private collection.

Author's website: www.FelicianoFinancial.com

ISBN 978-0-9847204-1-5 (Paperback)
ISBN 978-0-9847204-2-2 (Hardcover)
ISBN 978-0-9847204-3-9 (Ebook)
ISBN 978-0-9847204-4-6 (Kindle)

Library of Congress Control Number: 2023908844

Jose, Jeff, family matriarch Edie, Juanita, and John Feliciano

Contents

Contents

Acknowledgements

People often say that one's success in life can be attributed in some way to their parents. For some, the challenge of having difficult or absent parents can inspire them to strive harder. In my case, two unique parents are the foundation for my communication skills and my desire to include everyone and help them become the best version of themselves. A wise man once taught me to "Just Be." Despite difficult circumstances, my father found the courage to be the best version of himself. My mother embodies dignity, grace, truth, and love. To both my parents, who gave me my third language, I offer my respect, gratitude, and love. Both of them being deaf, they have always been far from silent! I take them with me wherever I go, beginning and ending each of my speeches in their language - one I share with love.

Knowing that I am supported by two remarkable people, I take their legacy of love and pay it forward.

To my wife Wanda, who believes in me and always has my back, and my daughter April, who puts my life into proper perspective every time I see her, I'd like to thank both my girls.

To John, who gave me everything he had to start my business, thank you for being everything a brother could want.

To Jeff, who allowed me to share his journey as an athlete and who shares with me every day as we build the business, thanks for playing "this game" with me.

To my sister Juanita, who makes sure the kid is alive and well in all of us, thank you for showing us where the magic lives. Like Mom, you have grace and love, and you know how to create a place called home.

To my other family, my thanks for your energy, commitment, loyalty, and for helping the Feliciano Financial Group grow into the best version of itself. Thanks for playing the game of life and running the marathon with me.

Finally, my thanks to all the speakers, consultants, and authors worldwide who preceded me. Many of you have paved my way and provided me with aspects of what has become a blueprint for my own success. I will do my best to pay forward the gifts you have given me.

"Cherish your visions and your dreams as they are the children of your soul, the blueprints of your ultimate achievements."
- Napoleon Hill

Jose Feliciano

From The Author

Success unshared doesn't do much. Paying it forward and sharing the steps along the way is as important as getting "there." I have stood on the shoulders of giants to get where I am today. This book is my steppingstone for those of you who don't want to reinvent the wheel.

If you believe a person can learn from their mistakes, but a smart person learns from other people's mistakes, then I invite you to borrow shamelessly from this book. I would be honored to know that something you read here might just give you an "aha" moment.

I learned that when the student is ready the mentor or teacher appears - sometimes even within the pages of a book.

"The place of my biggest challenge is always the source of my greatest strength."

Just Be

*"To be yourself in a world that is constantly trying to make you
something else is the greatest accomplishment."*
- Ralph Waldo Emerson

I am the oldest of four children, born to an immigrant Puerto
Rican father and a German-Irish mother, both of whom
were deaf. Of all the many life lessons they taught me over
the years, I always begin my professional speaking engagements
by repeating, in sign language, the one lesson by example that
my parents taught me every day of their lives: The place of my
greatest challenge is the source of my greatest strength.

My father, who was born deaf in Aquadilla, Puerto Rico, left
school in the sixth grade after his parents divorced. My pater-
nal grandfather owned a very successful paint and body shop in
Aquadilla and instinctively understood that when someone loses
one of their senses, the other senses will usually get stronger and
compensate for the loss. He also realized that, even at an early
age, my father was adept at working with his hands and patiently
taught him the life skills of the automobile painting and body

work business.

At the age of 19, my father left Puerto Rico and moved to a village slightly larger than his hometown of Aquadilla: New York City. He eventually found his mother and, using the skills he had learned as a boy, quickly got a job at a local paint and body shop in the city. During the day, he worked harder than anyone else in the shop, often covered from head to toe with auto paint and grease. But at five o'clock, he would get cleaned up, put on a suit and tie and one of those big old hats that were so popular in the 1950s, and go out to paint the town.

My mother, on the other hand, was a shy girl born and raised in the heart of New York City and, like my father, was also born deaf. She grew up in a rough section of New York called Hell's Kitchen, a collection of immigrant neighborhoods just north of the theater district.

It was a difficult life, but my mother never saw it that way. When I was a kid, I asked her why our neighborhood was called Hell's Kitchen, and she told me that it was shorthand for going to Hellmuth's Restaurant on the corner. She explained that rather than people saying they were going to Hellmuth's Restaurant for breakfast, they would simply say they were going to Hell's Kitchen. Between you and me, there was no Hellmuth Restaurant in the 1800s when a reporter for the New York Times first referred to that section of the city as Hell's Kitchen - but my mom has never been able to see the negative side of life. Even though I told her the real origin of the name and corrected her years ago, if you were to ask her today about Hell's Kitchen, she would more than likely tell you how everyone in New York used to go for breakfast at the Hellmuth Restaurant on the corner.

Brothers John and Jose Feliciano outside NYC apartment circa 1968

She still always finds the positive in life.

Now, as fate would have it, my soon-to-be parents met at a city-wide bowling tournament held for over 200 hearing-impaired adults in New York. They dated for about a year, got married, and the next thing you know, a year later they had me, Jose Anselmo Feliciano Jr.

Life wasn't easy for a deaf couple living on 47th Street in New York City with a brand new baby boy. Talk about overcoming life's obstacles! A few years ago, I asked my mother how she knew when I would cry at night. She explained that, because babies kick their feet when they cry, all she had to do was lay me sideways next to her in bed and the kicking from the crying would wake her up. I don't think anyone ever taught my mother that little trick, but we all learn to adapt in our own way.

My grandparents, my mother's parents Tim and Edith, lived in the apartment below us, and my grandfather was the superintendent of the building we lived in. They were the ones who taught me to speak, and by the time I was five years old, I had become my parents' most reliable interpreter, which in turn bonded us together in more than just the usual parent-child relationship.

It's funny, years ago I remember telling my daughter April, like we all do, not to speak with strangers. But when I said those words, I realized how different a world we all live in nowadays. I grew up talking to strangers for my parents; it was a way of life. I had to learn quickly how to understand adult words and thoughts, and then figure out a way to communicate that information to my parents using the limited vocabulary of a five-year-old.

More than a few years ago, my daughter asked a brilliant question: "If I don't talk to strangers, Daddy, how do I meet new people?" There is really no good answer to that question, is there? That's one of the great things about having kids around; they ask simple, uncensored questions that make us think and sometimes answer outside our comfort zone. I remember when we were living in New York; we couldn't go to the apartments of people we didn't know, but that didn't put a damper on Halloween. Instead of going from door to door, we would put on our costumes and, in groups of two or three, walk up to perfect strangers and yell "Trick or treat!" We must have been very cute kids all dressed up like that, because almost everyone we went up to would reach into their coats and put whatever pocket change they could find into our bags. On a good year, we could each clear fifteen to twenty dollars. The more entrepreneurial among us - the kids in the neighborhood who learned early to think outside the box—would also dress up on the day before Halloween to take advantage of all the tourists who weren't really sure what day it was. Twenty-five or thirty dollars bought an awful lot of candy in those days.

When I was 12 years old, my parents and I attended a parent-teacher conference at my school, P.S. 51. This is the first time I remember being embarrassed by my parents - it was a kid thing. Our sixth-grade teacher, Miss Horn, was at the front of the room talking about the new school year. My best friend Bobby was over there with his mom and dad, and right in front of me with her parents was the object of my first schoolboy crush, Becky.

Even though my job that night was to interpret for my parents, I must have been distracted and stopped paying attention for a few seconds. Suddenly, my father tapped me on the shoulder and asked what the teacher was saying. Being a typical 12-year-old, I signed back that I would tell him later, which I guess only frustrated him even more than not being able to hear. To get my attention again and to make sure I understood he was more than a little annoyed with me, my father clapped his hands once, very loudly, and asked again in sign language, "What is your teacher saying?"

Before I could answer him, I realized that everyone in the room had turned around and was looking in our direction. Then, to make matters worse, the teacher stopped talking and asked if there was a problem. I explained that my parents were deaf, and that my father was asking me what you were talking about. Talk about embarrassing!

Well, she waited until I, with everyone in the class watching, told my parents what they had missed. My face must have been bright red, and all I really remember is praying, over and over again, that the conference would end quickly.

When we got home that night, my father was upset and, before I went to bed, signed two words to me that I really didn't understand at the time. Two words that he would repeat more than a few times over the next few years. He said, "Jose. Just be."

Just be? Now I didn't have a clue what he meant by just be, but I was so happy to have survived the ordeal, I said "O.K." and quickly went off to bed.

When I was fourteen, my family packed up everything that would fit into a few old suitcases and sold everything else that we couldn't carry. My parents, my two brothers, my sister, and I all went down to the Port Authority Terminal, bought six bus tickets, and boarded a Trailways Bus for Jacksonville, Florida.

We were moving from Hell's Kitchen in New York City to Jacksonville, Florida. Jacksonville! Can you imagine how excited I was? Goodbye to New York's cold, snowy winters, hello to Jacksonville's beautiful, warm, sandy beaches. I was going to be living in a year-round paradise of endless summers, bikinis, and sun tan lotion. I was the luckiest 14-year-old in the history of the world!

Well, Jacksonville WAS sunny and hot. But there were no beaches to be found. You see, I guess in the excitement of hearing we were moving to Jacksonville, I didn't realize that in addition to Jacksonville, Florida, there is also a town called Jacksonville in Texas.

Jacksonville, Texas? It turns out we were moving from a city of seven- million people to a very small town in Texas with a population of seven- thousand people, 111 miles southeast of Dallas on U.S. 175.

From a city with thousands of taxi cabs to a town with only one cab driver - and he wasn't even busy. From the city so nice they named it twice to the Tomato Capital of the World. From the concrete jungle and pizza by the slice to the wide open spaces and taco stands.

From the big apple to the small tomato. I could go on like this all day, but I think you get the idea. Now, if you know anything about Texas, you know that football is king! My dream was to go to the University of Texas in Austin. All my friends were going there and the campus was full of pretty girls. There are 80,000 fans at each home football game, and the school also offers a great education.

Reality set in when I was 18 and I had to make the choice of either becoming the legal guardian of my brother and sister or letting them go to foster care. Then I thought about my parents, both of whom were deaf and mute, and my father with a sixth-grade education in Spanish. They had to overcome obstacles on a daily basis that we all take for granted, such as how to get from point A to point B in a city like New York City without being able to talk or even hear the directions.

How do you get a job without being able to talk at the interview, and if you get that job, how do you keep it when you can't even hear what your job is or what your fellow workers are trying to say to you? Furthermore, how do you even find an apartment? I realized that if my parents could overcome obstacles like that every day of their lives, becoming my brother and sister's legal guardian at 18 would be a snap.

The day after my high school graduation, I got a job flagging for a road construction company. Standing in the hot sun, I thought about making enough money to buy some form of transportation and pondered my future. Over the summer, I saved $1,000 and bought an old 1967 Chevy Impala - the kind of car they liked in *Goodfellas*, with a trunk large enough to give a couple of your deceased friends a ride to the dump. At the end of the summer, I left the road crew and got a job at Montgomery Ward, and registered for classes at the local community college.

So there I was, driving my $600 Impala, legal guardian of my brother and sister, working 30 hours a week at Montgomery Ward selling appliances I couldn't afford, taking 18 hours of classes at the local community college, paying my way through school, living in a painfully small one-bedroom apartment, interpreting for my parents, and, for good measure, I had decided to join a fraternity.

Before I knew what had happened, a few of my fraternity brothers had nominated me for president of the chapter. My opponent was a pledge brother who came from a wealthy neighborhood in Dallas, Highland Park, with a four-car garage, a gardener, and a brand-new Datsun 280 ZX, the sports car of sports cars. In town, he had a two-bedroom apartment, didn't have to work, always had a wad of cash in his pocket, and his tuition was paid in full.

When I looked at him and then at myself, I realized there was no way I could win. As I considered our respective backgrounds, I even thought about voting for him. When they announced that Jose Feliciano was the president of the Sigma Epsilon fraternity for the next year, everything went quiet and I suddenly realized what my dad had been telling me all along: "Stop worrying about what everyone else thinks. Just be. Don't try to be someone else, just be the best version of yourself you can be."

At that moment, I understood the words of Mark Twain who said, "When I was fourteen, my father was so ignorant I could hardly stand to have the old man around. But when I got to be twenty-one, I was astonished at how much the old man had learned in seven years."

You see, it turns out that the same parents I was embarrassed about when I was twelve, because they were different, because they were deaf, were the same people who taught me the most powerful lessons of my life. I had always had love, family, and friendships, but they taught me by example to be caring and considerate. They taught me to be a leader and to stop worrying about what everyone else thinks and just be.

Never Taking Life's Gifts for Granted

"Let us be grateful to the people who make us happy; they are the charming gardeners who make our souls blossom."
- Marcel Proust.

By the time I was nineteen, I had worked my way up to the top sales position in appliances at Montgomery Ward. I felt like I was king of the world. Although many of the people I worked with were twice my age, customer service came more naturally to me than it did to most. I also had a great command of brand names from dishwashers to electric stoves. My family's financial security was assured.

Or so I thought.

It turns out that reaching that level of success and responsibility at such a young age was not the best thing that could have happened. However, what I learned as a result of occasionally sleeping in late turned out to be a valuable life lesson.

As the star salesman, I started showing up for work after everyone else had clocked in for the day. I was a college student, burning the candle at both ends, trying to earn money and take a full load of credits. I knew I should be on time, but I told myself, "I am the number one sales guy. What are they going to say to me?" Soon, my one-hour lunch stretched into an hour and a half. I would come in, ready to hit the floor and make some sales, yet I was still half an hour later than everyone else on the team. "There is no way they are going to let me go," I kept telling myself. "They need me, so what difference does thirty minutes make?" I soon found out.

They fired me.

I was absolutely shocked. I couldn't afford to be without a job, so I went to my professor in petroleum engineering (I was majoring in petroleum engineering at the time) and asked him if anyone in the oil business was hiring. He told me to contact two of his friends in offshore drilling down in New Orleans, several hours away. After a long, lonely drive to New Orleans (only to find out they weren't hiring), I was in a quandary.

I was working to support my younger siblings and help my mom. As I drove back home to Texas, I was desperate and down to my last twenty dollars. Somewhere around Beaumont with several hundred miles to go, I made a phone call. It was one of the most difficult conversations I have ever had, but one that changed my future.

I called my former boss; the quarters stuck to my sweaty hand as I deposited them into the payphone and dialed the store. While they transferred me to my supervisor's desk, I

took a deep breath and considered what I would say.

"Hello?" The woman's voice came over the line.

"Hi, it's Jose," I said in my most upbeat voice. There was a long silence. "Do you believe in learning from mistakes?" I asked. There was an even longer silence.

Fortunately, my supervisor eventually said that yes, she did believe in learning from mistakes. I promised her that if she allowed me to have my old job back, I would be punctual and I would never take advantage of the situation again. Would she consider speaking to me?

By the time I hung up, I had made an appointment with her for Monday morning. However, it was Friday and as I rolled back into the parking lot of my apartment complex, I knew I had another difficult conversation ahead of me, as I had no money left to pay my rent.

I walked into the rental office to speak with the landlord. A few minutes later, I left and went straight to my apartment. I put on an old t-shirt and jeans, then walked outside to the maintenance garage and pulled out a red, greasy-handled push lawn mower. It took some convincing, but the landlord agreed to accept my rent later that month if I mowed the lawn and did some odd jobs around the complex over the weekend.

Not surprisingly, I had to work in a different department when I returned to Montgomery Ward on Monday. It hurt me that I couldn't go back to the appliance department that I knew so well. However, my attitude had changed. Before I lost my job, I had taken advantage of my position. The company couldn't do without me. Now, I knew differently.

Approach Life as a Gift

I guess we all fail to appreciate all that we have until the moment we are in danger of losing it. What is most important in life we tend to take for granted-from our relationships, to our jobs, to our homes. We get so busy making a living that we forget how precious life is.

Karl Wallenda, the patriarch of the tightrope act The Great Wallendas, once said, "Being on the tightrope is living; everything else is waiting." Once you experience what you know in your heart is "really living," it becomes impossible to take another moment for granted.

You can imagine, of course, that Karl Wallenda never arrived late to a tightrope performance. He never shirked his responsibilities or gave what he was doing half of his attention. He could not afford to. This immigrant circus performer knew that life was a precious gift because he was in danger of losing it every day. He had the privilege of living (and, ironically, dying) doing what he loved every day. If you are not doing whatever that is, you have neither found your place, nor fully realized that life is a gift.

Appreciate Today

Part of the problem is that we spend so much of today waiting for tomorrow. When it's winter, we can't wait for spring to arrive. After a few months of spring and summer, all we can think about is when it will cool off. We wait for someone's call, we wait for our next raise, and we long for our next vacation. Meanwhile, life is busy happening all around us.

When we are so focused on waiting for tomorrow to arrive, we begin to take for granted all that we have today. Having a passion for possibility means we are constantly thinking about and planning for the future, while still being firmly rooted in the present.

Let's take business as an example. Some companies start looking for new business all the time when they should be taking care of their current clients. Your existing clients are the lifeblood of your business, not the new group you are trying to attract. If you take care of people, they will take care of you as well.

In my business, we constantly focus on appreciating what we have now and strengthening those relationships.

I have an expanded definition of client; I look at my employees and vendors as clients too. If I take the time to nurture all of these relationships today with the same special care and attention I would give to a client, tomorrow will take care of itself.

Jimmy Durante once quipped, "Be nice to people on your way up, because you'll meet them again on your way down."

When you believe that anything is possible in your future, you view people differently. Every relationship gains greater significance. Consider the young college student at the front desk of your gym. Suppose that every time you see him, you strike up a conversation and ask him how it's going at school. You treat him with kindness and respect. It's possible that fifteen years later, he could be the next HR manager for a huge company that wants to do business with you - all because this young man remembers how you treated him.

When I teach young people at Junior Achievement, I often ask them, "Do you know someone who loaned you five dollars that you didn't repay, or perhaps you loaned someone five dollars and they didn't pay you back?" The kids usually look around and laugh nervously, as they all have been in that situation. I then say, "Do you realize that if you don't pay someone back, you're making a statement about who you will be in 20 years?"

Now that I have their attention, I explain, "That person who loaned you money that you did not pay back? They will grow up knowing not to do business with you because you showed them what kind of person you are."

Everything you do today affects tomorrow. When you learn to appreciate everything and everyone in your life, you open yourself up to potential blessings down the road. Relationships are exponential and far-reaching; each has the potential for positive results in the future. You never know where one act of kindness or generosity will lead.

Not Taking Relationships for Granted

Once people graduate from college, they don't stay in

touch. It's as if they can easily move away from friendships, but I never could do that. I have made a determined effort to remain reasonably connected with 90% of the friendships I had 20-30 years ago.

When I graduated from college, I knew everyone would start drifting apart once they had their own families and children. I wanted to create an event where my fraternity brothers and their wives and families would come back together to celebrate each year. There wasn't much to do in Tyler at that time, so two days before New Year's Eve the year after graduation, everyone contributed five dollars to organize the first of many annual New Year's parties.

Because I chose to stay in Tyler and build my family and business in this community, I also developed new relationships. Soon, this small gathering of fraternity brothers grew into a Tyler New Year's celebration event that included hundreds of people! Every year for 20 years, people came from all over to dress up, dance, and create New Year's Eve memories. In later years, we even had to rent a community hall when 800 people showed up one year, all dressed in formal wear. It was incredible.

One of the best things about the party was the fact that everyone paid their own way, especially when hundreds of people were involved. I have never believed that anyone fully appreciates a free lunch when they would rather do their part. The best parties are not necessarily the high-dollar affairs where everything is catered; some of the most memorable get-togethers occur when everyone contributes. That annual event taught me not to take life for granted. It was a time to appreciate all of the relationships God had given us and celebrate that together.

Priorities Change

Of course, priorities change. After nineteen years of this annual tradition, my daughter came to us two weeks before the party and asked, "Mom and Dad, when can I spend New Year's with you?" She was ten years old at the time. My wife smiled and said, "When you're twenty-one, you can come," (knowing that a ten-year-old would not have much fun at a formal dance for adults). My daughter looked hurt and said, "You mean I have to wait eleven more years to celebrate New Year's with my parents?"

I realized she was right.

I told my family that we would not have a party the following year and that we would spend New Year's Eve together as a family. The next year, we celebrated the stroke of midnight out at sea, under the stars, aboard a cruise ship.

I still value the friendships with those from my fraternity. Now, I host family functions that include all of their families as well as mine. I had to find a way to value my expanded circle of friends, and I still don't take any of them for granted.

Appreciating Life Means Being Teachable

When I was coaching Senior League, one of my best players was a fifteen-year-old with the worst work habits I had ever seen. At practice, I would catch him slacking off in the outfield, relaxing on one knee. The kid was talented - more talented than any of his peers because he had matured faster - but I could tell by the look on his face that he was thinking, "What's the point?"

Inevitably, the other kids noticed and they also began to

slack off. Not only did I have a responsibility to help this player overcome his laziness, I felt like the whole team was suffering as a result.

I did something radical: I benched my best player for the next three games. When one person breaks the rules and falls short of expectations, it affects everyone else. Team morale is found anywhere groups of people work together, whether it be a church, a business, a family, or a junior league.

The boy's father came to me all upset about my decision to bench his son. I stood my ground and told him that it was going to be the best lesson for him. If I let him shirk his responsibility to the team, even though he was good, it would just reinforce lazy work habits that would follow him all his life. "He'll be done for good," I tried telling the angry father (who also happened to be a friend and client). He wasn't convinced and walked off in disagreement.

If this were not a true story, I would say that the kid shaped up for the next game, rallied his teammates, apologized profusely, and was a different kid from that day forward. However, things did not happen that way.

He quit.

After being benched for the third time, my best player walked. I wanted to teach him and the other kids on the team that we had to treat practice as if it were a game situation, as life does not give us practice tries; it is the real thing.

He eventually called me up, apologized, and told me he would change his attitude. In fact, he went further than anyone else in the league. Today, he still thanks me for the splinters in his backside that he got from sitting on the bench for all those games.

College scouts don't necessarily look at what you do on game day; they want to see your work ethic in practice. They want to know one thing: no matter how good you may be or how talented you are, are you coachable? They would rather have someone who is coachable than someone who thinks they know it all, as an attitude like that will damage the team culture. People can get comfortable just getting by; they may be at the top of their game for a while, but taking that position for granted always leads to negative results.

Assumption is the Enemy of Appreciation

When I became the legal guardian of my younger siblings, they were 6 and 4 years old. Early on, I sat down with them at the kitchen table at our mother's house and asked them point blank what they expected of me. We had to be more grown up than most people our age at the time, so they took this conversation seriously.

They started giving me a list that included things like paying the rent for Mom, making sure they were taken care of, and providing food on the table. As a college student working and going to school full time, I explained to them that if I didn't work and follow my obligations, I would lose the family home. I showed them how bills worked and the ins and outs of running a household.

Next, I asked them what I should expect from them. They suggested doing their part around the house, getting good grades, picking up after themselves, respecting their mother, going to bed on time - all the things that they could control.

I wrote two lists in two separate columns on a legal pad. Once we looked over that piece of notebook paper, we all

Edie, John, Jose, Juanita, Jeff, and Jose Feliciano Sr.

three signed it as if it were a legal document. It was a huge lesson for them and a significant turning point for me in understanding the value of clear communication. Everyone understood their role in the future success of our family and no one assumed what the others would do, in order to guard against taking each other for granted. One of the greatest challenges I faced as the new head of my family was dealing with this very issue.

When my younger sister was seventeen years old, she worked in my office, answering the phone and doing odd jobs. As her guardian and head of the family, I paid for family expenses, such as the insurance on her car. Typical of a high school student, she didn't take her job working for her big brother seriously. She was chronically late and would go to her cubicle, in front of the other employees, thirty or forty-five minutes past the hour.

21

I called her into my office one day and told her that if she was late one more time, I would have to let her go. That would mean no more gas money, no more paying for insurance premiums, nothing.

A few days later, she was late again. I will never forget the look of shock on her face when I told her to pack up her desk and go home.

I cut off her insurance and gas money and didn't give her a dime from that day onward. It was the hardest thing I have ever had to do.

I thought she expected me to come around in a few days when she saw how she was struggling. However, after a month, she knew I was serious. She applied at a nearby fast food restaurant and started working there. Would you believe that this teenager, who couldn't be on time anywhere, soon became employee of the month?

Later, she found a better-paying job at an equipment company and was a model employee; she was up at seven in the morning and was never late. Years later, when she came back to work with us at the firm, she was a different person.

Assumption is the enemy of appreciation. We don't appreciate what we take for granted. People often don't appreciate their job until they lose it and have to look for work. Similarly, they often don't appreciate good health until something goes wrong.

The moment we start making assumptions about the permanence of a relationship, a job, or our health, we begin to devalue it. Loss sometimes acts as the jolt we need to stir us from our assumptions.

Life's Best Gifts Often Come in Disguise

Sometimes I forget that my negative experiences contain gifts. What I initially thought were the worst experiences in my life have turned out to be the best thing that could have happened.

I coached my little brother Jeff's Senior League baseball team when he was around fifteen years old. There was a play at the plate and, amid a huge cloud of dust, the umpire stepped forward and yelled at my player, "You're OUT!" However, the player was actually safe.

During the next inning, Jeff was warming up on the pitcher's mound when he overheard the home plate umpire admitting to the second base umpire, "Man, I really blew that last call."

I was standing in the dugout watching Jeff when suddenly he began using sign language to tell me exactly what the umpires were saying! Nobody else knew what Jeff was doing, so I made my way onto the field and up to the home plate umpire.

"So you know you blew the call?" I said to him, I will never forget the look on his face.

Seeing the umpire hem and haw was worth every minute of growing up with deaf parents. I wish I had a nickel for every time I resented having to speak sign language as a young kid. You don't always feel appreciative of everything that happens in life, especially when you're convinced you've gotten a raw deal. Of course, that umpire never admitted he threw the call; he threw me out of the game instead! But I smiled all the way back to the bench.

When you react to life's challenges with negativity, what can you expect to happen other than more disappointment and negative outcomes?

Look for Moments to Celebrate

When you look at life from a positive perspective, you will always find something to celebrate, and celebration is the fuel that keeps us going. We need to acknowledge every milestone along the way. Every time I finish what I have set out to do, I take time to fully appreciate the step before eyeing the next goal.

Doubt

"The only limit to our realization of tomorrow will be our doubts of today."
—Franklin D. Roosevelt

So many of us spend a lot of time worrying about what people think of us, which can prevent us from being who we truly are and from doing the things we really want to do. It can stop us from making bold choices and taking risks.

As I look back on college, the one thing I didn't count on was the overwhelming thoughts of self-doubt. But I always remembered seeing my father tell me, "Jose, stop worrying about what other people think. Just be." Whenever self-doubt began to rear its ugly head, I could hear my father's words, "Jose, stop worrying about what other people think. Just be."

So I took "Just Be" everywhere I went. "Just be" evolved into "Be, Do, Have." Be the person you want to be, do the things you need to do, and you'll have the things you want to have. However, "Be" was always at the top of my list. It kept my priorities straight and kept me centered.

If you cannot feel it and be with it, you cannot even begin to think about undertaking the journey. When you can see things done and your objectives are clear, you will not be swayed by detours or the hiccups in the road along the process -- you can stay the course because you know where you are going.

With the destination in mind, life becomes an adventure, filled with lessons, family, children, gifts, and challenges that often turn out to be gifts in disguise. If you had said that Jose from New York, with two deaf parents and a beat-up Chevy Impala, would have looked to the future logically and thought about success, I would have said, "No way, Jose."

But, "Just be," that evolved into, "be, do, have," allowed me to dream and leave the doubts behind me.

I learned a long time ago that doubt is the enemy, not fear. Doubt is the father of all negative emotions and the thief who steals our dreams and makes us play it safe. We may think that if we are sure about our vision and destination, people will find us cocky or self-centered. However, doubt just brings out the worst in each of us. It kills the magnificent. Doubt says, "It can't be done. It's impossible."

More recently, I have learned to respect my ally, doubt, because I have begun to discover the strange truth about him. Doubt actually holds a secret in his hands. I began to realize that he is the guardian of the gates to all miracles. Doubt asks to be overcome, and by overcoming doubt, it paves new ways, creates new rules, establishes new limits, and sets new records. Doubt is the wise guardian that challenges the very best to step forward for each one of us, if we are prepared to look it in the face and say, "I respect you, I know your value, but I am moving past you."

More recently, I have learned to respect my ally, doubt. I have also begun taking doubt on as an advisor, because doubt will show you where the potential pitfalls are. It will point out those who aren't on board with your vision. Which, in turn, tells you where you need to spend a little more energy or add a little more clarity.

As the legal guardian of my siblings by the age of 18, I had to learn to get past doubt quickly and move on to believing. Then, you have to get beyond believing into knowing that everyone will succeed. If I had even thought about the challenges, I would have been overwhelmed.

As we built the Feliciano Financial Group, "do" came alongside to play with "be." We had to do our homework, working in and on our business every day, always being and doing with the end in mind.

168 Hours

"Time is what we want most, but what we use worst."
- William Penn

There are 168 hours in a week, on average 56 of which are spent sleeping, leaving us with 112 hours to work with. We are fortunate to be living in a world where technology has made us more productive.

Rapid transportation has not created more time, but it has given us back some of the time we would have spent getting to and from places.

Similarly, the Internet has not created more time, but it has given us back some of the time we would have spent doing research and accessing important materials, by allowing us to communicate with our family, friends, and clients instantly with the touch of a button.

Despite all this newfound efficiency, we all seem to be busier than ever.

Our quality of life is a direct reflection of how we choose to spend our 168 hours each week. Despite all the technical

and social advancements of the last five hundred years, one thing has remained constant: we must prioritize. We have to decide how to spend our time, focusing on the more important things in life rather than the less important. However, no matter how carefully we prioritize, many of us will look back and think, "If only I had known then what I know now, I would have chosen to spend my time differently."

When our values are clear, our decisions are easier. You know, Dr. Stephen Covey, the author of *The Seven Habits of Highly Effective People*, wrote, "The enemy of the best is often the good." There are so many ways to spend our time, and the quality of our life is the best when we choose to spend time engaged in the best things. Whenever possible, delegate at least some of those things that are less important to the quality of our life to someone else.

Taking money out of the mix, what is most important to

you? Faith and spirituality? It cannot be delegated.

What about our health? Just because we can hire a personal trainer at $75 an hour doesn't mean that getting healthy can be delegated. Spending $500 an hour on a personal trainer still doesn't get the job done either. Now, you would think that for $1,000 an hour we could get some satisfaction, but we are still the ones that have to sweat. We need to take responsibility for exercising and keeping a healthy diet. So, since we can't delegate our health, we need to decide how important it is to us and how many of our 168 hours each week we're willing to spend on it. Family? Well, some people try. But we can't hire a nanny to raise our kids to love us. And even though we try to justify our choices by saying that it's okay because we're spending "quality time" together, it's really just an excuse to help us feel better about ourselves and avoid admitting to ourselves that we're too busy to recognize the real priorities in our life. We would all like to spend more hours each week, maybe many more hours each week than we currently do, being with and enjoying family and friends and the people we care most about. But we have to make the effort and conscious choice to find the time, to dedicate some of our 168 hours each week to real quality time.

How about having fun? Can this be delegated? Who among us is willing to pay someone else to go on vacation and have fun for them? Here's $5,000 - go on vacation for me and send me a postcard to let me know how much fun you had. If you know someone like that, send them my way; I'll take the $5,000 and their vacation for them and promise to send a postcard. In fact, if they can come up with

$15,000, I'll take my wife and daughter along and promise they'll send a postcard from Hawaii too.

We can all find the time for everything that is most important to us. We just need to prioritize and use smart delegation.

Envisioning Your Goals

"A goal without a plan is just a wish."
- Antoine de Saint-Exupéry

On my way to the university for my scheduled speech, I couldn't help but appreciate the captivating beauty of the spring morning. Tyler, Texas showcased its potential with blooming crepe myrtles, a fitting metaphor for the bright and enthusiastic students I was about to engage with. As I reviewed my notes, I took a moment to carefully consider the impending speech, ensuring it aligned with my intended message and purpose. As a Certified Financial Planner and owner of a Wealth Management firm, addressing a graduating class in finance, I knew I could discuss the intricacies of the financial world that they were so anxious to enter. However, my heart kept prompting me to talk about something else altogether. What could I teach these students that would possibly stick with them more than just another speech about financial planning?

An image of a marathon sprang to mind. I am not a long-distance runner by any means, nor am I necessarily interested in becoming one anytime soon. However, a few weeks before, I had experienced a marathon through the eyes of an avid runner. One of my co-workers had invited our family to watch his wife run the White Rock Lake marathon near Dallas. As my brother and I waited at the finish line, along with several hundred other faithful friends and family members of the runners, I was amazed by what I saw. The excitement was palpable, as each exhausted runner crossed the finish line. Some panted with their hands on their hips as they slowed to a walking pace, while others slowed and fell into the arms of their waiting loved ones, who embraced them and cheered.

From my vantage point, I could see the runners making their way to the finish line for at least half a mile. As they approached the last leg of their journey, their faces showed that all of them were in the zone; nothing else mattered except crossing that finish line. A giant digital clock nearby counted off tenths of seconds, and some of them had their eye on that second hand, desperately hoping to beat their best time. Yet the majority just seemed focused on taking the next step forward; the rest of the runners around them didn't even seem to exist. It was intense, and I was just observing all of it from the sidelines!

I talk to people about their values and goals all day long. In my line of work, you quickly realize how much easier it is for people to make smart choices - with their money and with their lives - when they have a clear picture of their ultimate goal. I am constantly amazed by the power of a clearly defined goal and choosing to get on the path toward that objective. In all my years of business, I had seldom seen a group of people so focused - channeling every last bit of energy they had, to achieve success - until that day at the marathon. As I drove home, one thought dominated my thoughts: *What would it take to run 26 miles?*

Twenty-six miles is a long time to keep running. However, it became clear to me that day that a marathon is actually a lot longer than just the 26 miles on pavement. I was stationed at the finish line, but my thoughts kept going back to the moment the race started. In a race, all the attention focuses on the finish line and who breaks the tape first, but I realized that the starting line was in some ways just as important. The starting line for these runners began a lot further back than just a piece of tape stretched across a street 26 miles earlier. It stretched back several months, maybe even a year or more. The day they first made the decision to run a marathon, long before the starting gun fired on the day of the race, was when the race actually began. It began the moment the alarm sounded in the darkness on the very first morning of training.

Likewise, the finish line represented more than the end of a long race; it was a celebration of the hundreds of hours they had spent training and preparing before race day, fulfilling a long-range plan to succeed. As I watched these runners, it occurred to me that anything worth doing in life begins the same way: with desires and goals followed by a plan and the passion to achieve them. Michael Gerber writes in his book, *The E-Myth*, about the surprising reason that most small businesses/personal goals fail: it's not because their dream is too big, but rather too small and too realistic, not big enough to sustain a meaningful life.

We need to clearly see where we want to go, envision what it will feel like to achieve that goal, and plan our way backward. Every successful runner has clearly envisioned what crossing the finish line would feel like before they ever set foot on the pavement. They have already imagined the excitement, the thrill, and the feeling of strength and invincibility. This vision drives them to come up with a plan to experience all that moment holds in store. You run a race from start to finish, but first you must envision it from finish to start and figure out all the steps it will take to get you where you want to be.

With these ideas churning in my head, I set aside the speech I had rehearsed, took a deep breath, and opened with an illustration of running the White Rock Lake Marathon. Then I asked, "What does it take to run a marathon?" The students started firing off answers: new shoes, eating right, athletic shorts, a running coach. Fifty different answers came flying across the room: "Start slowly, build a timeline, exercise." About the time that some of the students probably started wondering what a marathon had to do with a career in finance, I asked them, "So, what is your 26 miles?"

The room became very quiet as I issued the challenge again, "What is your 26 miles?"

Here were all these students on the threshold of a new beginning, with the whole world open to them. They could run any "marathon" (a metaphor for what they wanted most out of life) that they wanted to. Some would run it in their hometown, working in the financial industry, marrying, having children, and buying their first home. Some would graduate and move to join a financial firm, possibly in Dallas, New York, or Boston, and begin a life there. As they anxiously paced the starting line of a brand-new life as soon-to-be college graduates, I wanted them to consider their goals carefully and picture the next finish line in their lives.

More importantly, I wanted them to visualize an important life goal and then start tracing back what it would take to get them there. I challenged them to realize that no matter what vision they had for their lives at that moment, once they had a specific destination in mind, they could begin their 26 miles. Every step they took toward this goal would count. (Incidentally, I had two students tell me that they wanted to run a real marathon after that!)

What's Your 26 Miles

So, what are your 26 miles? What specific goals do you want to achieve in your lifetime? Those things that keep you up at night thinking, "If money and practicality were not considerations, I'd be doing this right now..." Can you clearly see what it will take for you to break the tape at that finish line? Or did you turn thirty, forty, or fifty and decide the race was over for you? Whatever your goals are for your life, can you envision everything you will have to do in order to make them happen? That's where developing a passion for the possibilities in life begins, and it has no age limits. The great thing about dreams is that they have no expiration date.

Once you create a goal and stretch the tape across the finish line in your mind, you begin to deal with everything else in your life from a new perspective. You start to figure out how all of your activities, endeavors, relationships, and priorities relate to achieving that goal.

This kind of inner vision springs from a burning desire to convert a dream into reality and turn dedication into success. It comes from passion. You have to be passionate about the unexplored possibilities in your life. If you have no desire to be or do more in your life, you probably can't see any goals on the horizon worth pursuing. The truth is, some people have this passion and others just don't. But where does it come from? And if we suspect that we weren't born with it, then what?

Seeing the Possibilities

Most people say, "Seeing is believing." We have it wrong; if you choose to believe it first, then your eyes will be opened to seeing the possibilities. What do we truly believe about our ability to do the impossible? Our lives are primarily shaped by the foundational beliefs we adopted as children. Sometimes what we envision for our lives is limited because people convinced us from an early age that we cannot do certain things or become certain people, and we agreed.

Somewhere along the way, we allow someone or something to stifle the flame of possibility in our lives. We all start with grand ideas and a belief that we can accomplish almost anything. However, life begins to wear down most of us at some point with its routines and requirements, not to mention all the 'can't do' language we are exposed to. Our concentration starts to dwindle and, along with it, many of our aspirations.

I felt the first flicker of possibility in the tenth grade when an insurance agent came to my house to discuss auto insurance with my parents. My parents are both deaf and mute and I was interpreting for them. I remember sitting across the table from him and admiring his ability to help families with key decisions. More importantly, I understood that by helping my family think wisely about our future and implement a well-organized plan, he was putting us in touch with the ability to dream and to make those dreams a reality. I didn't necessarily want to be in the insurance business, but I knew after that night that I wanted to help people make wise decisions about the areas of their lives that were important to them.

The Rat Race or Your Race

You may have started your 26-mile marathon a long time ago with the finish line clearly in view. You had goals, dreams, and ideas. Then something happened; you got distracted by the stuff of life - changing jobs, marrying, moving cross-country, having kids, paying a mortgage, etc. You lost sight of the goal, and now life is just dragging you along. You are not living your life on purpose because you no longer believe that everything is possible. When we stop believing that everything is possible, we can no longer see it happening. The dream fades, and sometimes it even seems to disappear from view. When that happens, instead of steadily running a marathon towards our greater goals and dreams, we end up running a directionless race without a goal or dream in sight.

If this is you, you are not alone. Many people find themselves on the sidelines; it has been so long since they actively pursued their goals that they are now more comfortable among the spectators than those striving in the race of life.

Have you noticed that spectators look and act differently than those in the race? They're dressed differently for one thing; they don't look like runners with their jeans and Saturday-morning sweatshirts, whereas people in the race have their game on, stripping down to the necessities for hitting their goal - shorts, shirt, and shoes. People in the crowd are relaxed and casual, cupping their lattes and talking and laughing with each other as the minutes turn into hours. By contrast, those in the race count every minute, and they have an intensity in their eyes that has long been missing from the crowd.

Ask a runner in the middle of a marathon what is most important to them and you will get a definitive answer. The runners know without a doubt what is most important to them. Ask the crowd, and you are likely to meet with hesitation. Ask again and you might see a mix of looks between wistful defeat and glimmers of hope. Those who do not know what they want out of life have no lens of enthusiasm through which to envision the journey from start to finish. Are you in the crowd, or are you in the race?

If you were to start training for a marathon tomorrow, you could read books and peruse magazines about basic training for marathons, but that would only get you so far. You would have to actually get out there and start running to make it happen. And what if you overlooked an important step? What if you started to veer off course?

Anyone who is serious about attaining a goal reaches a critical turning point when they realize that they cannot go it alone. They must assemble a team that is willing to support their dream with passion. A focused group that can see the biggest picture possible and help them figure out every single thing that needs to take place all the way to the finish line. For a runner, this team might include other running partners, a nutritionist, or a coach. Friends and family members may be on the sidelines cheering them on. These people keep the athlete's eyes on the road when their focus starts to slip, continually charting the course toward the final goal.

Another strategic part of your 26-mile journey is to surround yourself with success. Begin by studying successful people in your community; make their acquaintance and examine their talents and achievements. You will undoubtedly uncover a support team of people standing behind the curtain; no successful person arrives at that place by themselves; they all need a team to help them get there.

You have to actively seek out others to help you construct the game plan and keep you on track. Hopefully, that is one of the reasons you picked up this book. Achieving the impossible is not just about achieving all that you can imagine for yourself; it is about creating and accessing allies who will motivate and assist you at critical points along the way. In fact, I devoted the last chapter of this book to "Surrounding Yourself with People Who Motivate" (Chapter 17).

There are plenty of resources; look for key people who know you, love you, and want the best for you. Good friends and close family members who believe in you, church groups and community organizations, teachers, mentors, and life coaches. Chances are, some of them will know at least one person who could play a key part in your success. Wisely choosing these people will help you take your life all the way to the top; your team is one of the most crucial choices you will ever make.

Of course, others can only be as enthusiastic about your dream as you are. If you are passionate and can envision it happening in your future, they will believe in it too. This chapter is about envisioning the impossible taking place in your life. I have found that there are key steps related to what I need to envision to achieve what I want:

You have to constantly envision where you are going, "feel" the picture, and never lose sight.

You have to visualize success happening in your future.

You have to identify and eliminate the self-imposed limits hindering your success.

Envision Where You're Going

The first step in any race is to envision where you are going and plot the journey to that destination. Athletes are single-mindedly focused on the goal at hand; even when they are training for a local track meet or a state championship, they always have something like the Olympics in mind - the grand picture. They always focus on the ultimate goal; everything else is subordinate to that ideal.

In my own race, I have always dreamed of making a global difference in the lives of children. One of the steps towards achieving this goal was being elected onto the school board by the age of 29. This way, I knew I could make choices that would have a positive impact on children. I came from a lower-income family and realized early on that education was my only way out. I have always wanted to motivate and encourage people to be the best version of themselves. In its own way, this book is a step towards fulfilling this goal, another way for me to have an impact or energize a life. And selfishly, this energizes me.

I had to learn the strategies for ignoring the distractions and overcoming challenges that threatened to take me off course, so I could pursue what was truly important to me. I needed a team of people to help me uncover my values, strengths, and desires in order to design a realistic yet ambitious plan for attaining those goals.

Furthermore, I had to learn to hold the vision I had in my mind; as Yogi Berra said in one of his famous Yogi-isms, *"You've got to be careful if you don't know where you're going, because you might not get there."*

I used to coach Little League football. Being in charge of 26 little kids running around with helmets so big they looked like bobble heads was quite a challenge! I remember one game when I huddled up with the offense to call the next play. Suddenly, I heard a little sniffle that rapidly escalated into muffled sobbing. My center had started crying in the middle of the huddle. I looked in his eyes and saw that he was scared of the bigger kids on the other team.

He was a little guy (all my guys were little), and he wasn't sure he wanted to go back to the line of scrimmage and play. I took him aside and I said, "Look. I know you're scared, and those other guys are a lot bigger than you. But you're smart. And smart beats strong." He kind of nodded his head and sniffed loudly again, but I could see the doubt in his eyes.

I knelt down on one knee and explained to him that he had an advantage over the others because he knew the snap count. "If you know when the snap count is," I told him, "then all you need to do is screen the defensive player from getting to where you know the ball is going. See? Knowledge is power." When I told him that he had the advantage because of what he knew, his face began to light up. He saw himself doing exactly what I described and winning. It gave him the strategy and vision he needed to succeed, and he did.

He was eight years old at the time, but even at such a young age he had raw talent. Something told me that if we hadn't had this little talk, he would have quit that day and never picked up a football again. Ten years later, this same kid became a great athlete and played middle linebacker for Texas A&M University.

Instead of picturing all that can go wrong, see yourself successfully making the leap from where you are now to where you want to be. Imagine what it looks like to thrive and picture yourself excelling.

Maybe it's been a long time since you experienced success in your personal life and you've forgotten what that feels or looks like. Maybe you've never known what it's like to reach for something beyond what you think you can attain and achieve it. For most people, that idea is a little intimidating. Fear of failure and nagging uncertainty about our futures are just two of the scavengers that eat away at our dreams and slyly keep us from daring to be, do, and have more in our lives. Chase those parasites away and envision yourself already there.

Becoming the Person You Dreamed You Could Be

"What you get by achieving your goals is not as important as what you become by achieving your goals."
- Zig Ziglar

Be, *Do* and *Have* in that order! Before you can do and have all that you imagine in life, you must first "be" willing to cultivate a strong character. Whenever you can do something to become a better version of yourself, it will have tremendous results. Often, we approach relationships with the idea of "What's in it for me?" Instead, we should ask, "How can I add value here?" Good investments lead to strong returns; this is true for everything you do in life. Financial investments require money to be carefully invested; character investments require investments of your second primary currency: time. There is always room to become a better person who does greater things. Remember: Be, Do, Have. You must first *be* the person you want to be in order to *do* what needs to be done so that you can *have* what you want.

I think we get it backwards many times. I hear people say, "If I had (some material item), I could be anyone I wanted to be," but that's not necessarily true. Modern advertising makes us feel as though we would be different people who are happier and more successful if we only had a certain product, but the products are only the perks, they are not a requirement.

Sure, some people may be drawn to a successful person because of what they may have, but it's the being part that keeps them there. A person's character can make you think that maybe, if you spend some time around them, whatever they have inside may rub off on you too. Knowing how to "just be" is crucial to success; that's why you have to "live it" before you can do it or have it.

Clarity of "being" comes next. If a mother says, "My goal is to raise good children and be a great wife," she is successful if she achieves that, regardless of what she has or does not have. You are the one who gets to define your own success. It is important that the image in your mind and the feeling inside of you align with what is in front of you.

Success for my wife means being a great wife and mother, and she is constantly focused on it, challenging herself in the area of personal growth. I believe that the hunger and pursuit of excellence in our lives is missing for too many of us, and yet it is the treasure map that leads to real fulfillment.

Business people often forget that they are selling themselves, not their product; that comes second. Realtors do not sell houses; they sell themselves. Pharmaceutical representatives don't sell medicines; they sell themselves. Our personal values, ideas, politics, worldviews, and religion all matter more and make a longer-lasting impression on people than what we do.

You Are Your Most Valuable Asset

It strikes me that we are careful to pass wealth and material goods from generation to generation, but equally careless when it comes to passing on family values to our children. If all they inherit is the money, they miss out on the real treasure-the character behind the story of how the wealth was accumulated. The real deal behind the success. Without that story, the money is incomplete, looking for a place to anchor. It's the story that creates a dynasty, a sense of respect for the characters who created incredible wealth and accumulated amazing stories of courage and perseverance along the way. Money is the byproduct; the story is the wealth.

Many successful people fail four or five times before they find their stride. The patriarch of a family may be a wealthy man today, but what people don't realize is that he may have won and lost a fortune two or three times before he achieved success.

The grandchildren think granddad always had it big, so they don't learn to participate in the adventure he has begun and add their own unique next chapter. They don't look at the man behind the money; all they see is the good life. Unless they add an episode or two of their own, they'll never be able to fully appreciate the fruits of his labor or make sure the next crop is ready for harvest. Worse yet, they may fail to inherit his strength and character along with the money;

that's like having the pie with no filling.

You may have heard the saying that once you become a millionaire, it is easy to become a millionaire again. There is some truth to that. After the first million, the millionaire has a map for what is required. They understand the rules and the equipment they need, including the character they have so carefully cultivated, is all in place. Now, all they have to do is duplicate the pattern. Who they became along the way is now worth many more millions of dollars. It might be a long journey to that second million, but this time, they are ready.

When people inherit money from the previous generation without the accompanying work ethic or the desire to succeed, statistics show that the real wealth has evaporated by the third generation.

In fact, today's statistics reveal that nearly 90% of all inheritances are gone within eighteen months.

Why is that? The money is passed on, but not the values. What we haven't earned or will not nurture, we have little chance of keeping. Therefore, communicating the family mission statement – clearly stated goals for the family that everyone can buy into - is something that we should all be doing from the day our children are old enough to hear it. If we set expectations for their part in it and look at positioning their strengths within the family business, we can confidently expect the next generation to run the organization after we have gone. We have to make sure they learn to develop those leadership skills and character qualities that brought success in the first place. That is our responsibility; it is part of growing a successful society, which is, after all, an extension of our business.

I created an interview process with my clients to walk people through the life lessons they have learned along the way. The response has been phenomenal, as people get a chance to help their kids inherit so much more than just dollars and cents. They want their descendants to know the family story and understand the family values. They want them to know what their great-grandfather was thinking when he had money, and when he lost money, how did that affect him and how did he make it back?

We develop character throughout our lives, but the process begins in our families. It starts from when we are small and lasts forever as we gain more and more experience. In my own family, I can identify different experiences where my parents took the opportunity to shape my character.

Challenges Develop Character

I remember the drive to the water department; I was only nine at the time, but I recall rehearsing in my mind exactly what I would say to the people in the office when we got there. My family had just moved to Jacksonville, Texas from Manhattan, and I had never seen so many green, grassy areas or such open spaces in my life.

I am a native New Yorker, but when I was growing up, the city was very different. Back then, I walked a few blocks from my family's residence to Public School #51 every day in the third grade. Now we were starting anew in a new city, in a completely different part of the country where they spoke much more slowly and said things like "Y'all."

As the oldest son, I had to help make some of the arrangements for our family's cross-country move from New York to Texas. And on this day, our first day in Jacksonville, we needed to arrange to have the electricity and utilities turned on so we could move in.

I understood how money worked because my parents would explain it to me using the checkbook register. I spoke with my parents about what needed to be done to set up services where we lived. As we walked into the water department that day, I'm sure it surprised the woman behind the front counter when she asked my parents, "How may I help you?" and they both turned to look at me. I learned to handle adult situations from a young age.

Growing Up Different is a Blessing

I received the gift of parents who, in their own way, expected me to be a leader at every opportunity and gave me ample circumstances to apply what I was learning. By the time I was 18, I had a full handle on the activities involved in daily family living. It created a lot of trust in our family and built my self-confidence. I knew more about family responsibilities than most students much older than me.

Sadly, many families do not involve their children in the day-to-day operations of the family, perpetuating ignorance and creating a lack of trust. It appears that a contributing factor to why some parents lack confidence in their children's ability to handle money is that they did not allow their children to be involved in the financial process while growing up. As a result, they never developed the mindset and skills necessary to comprehend the value and role of money in the family. It is ironic how we sometimes unintentionally create the very scenarios we were most trying to avoid.

As I lead families through financial and life planning, I have noticed that parents who are open with their children tend to be much closer emotionally. There seems to be a lot more trust between members of the family. Oftentimes in families like these, the assets have a better chance of surviving from generation to generation because parents have taken the time to teach the children about value and how money works. The kids also know the story behind the wealth; they inherit it all.

On the other hand, there are parents who do not trust their children to handle the family finances. These parents often do not realize how they contributed long ago to their adult children's inability to function in a world of finance, relationships, and personal values. The stalemate in communication permeates the family, and the adult children are directionless because they were never included in the decision-making process.

No one develops character in a vacuum. It is amazing how much we contribute to developing each other's character - enhancing it or depleting it - through some of the little things we do or do not do.

I don't think my parents ever fully understood that they were doing me a favor by involving me in family responsibilities that many people would have considered too much for a child to handle. When you're deaf coming into a hearing world, there is a lot more you have to do just to survive. I watched my parents do more than survive; they raised a family and taught me that anyone can make it.

Praising Someone's Character Every Chance You Get

Does character matter if you get the job done? To me, it is the only way to get the job done. It matters in everything that you do. It requires that you evaluate your own life and lead by example. Character raises the standard everywhere; it is often underrated yet crucial for lasting success.

Sadly, we do not recognize it enough in our homes, offices, and communities. We forget to acknowledge positive character traits in others, instead of citing their shortcomings.

It is one thing to see strength of character in an individual and another to recognize it. We may observe compassion and dependability in others, but we seldom go the extra mile to acknowledge or honor the quality we observe.

We are so caught up in recognizing accomplishments that we forget to acknowledge quality and character strengths. For example, we could say to someone, "Thank you for getting those notes to me before my meeting." That is recognizing what someone did to contribute to a smooth office environment, and it is important. However, I would rather say to the person who brought me the notes, "Your dependability allows this team to function well; I am grateful that I can rely on you."

It's the difference between showing gratitude for what people do and expressing appreciation for who they are. Showing gratitude is almost compulsory and can be accomplished by a simple "thank you." I'm guessing that we probably don't even practice this simple step enough; we don't write enough thank you notes, and we overlook making that extra phone call to tell someone that we're grateful.

When we express sincere appreciation, we go beyond what they do for us and touch on who they are. Whereas gratitude is generally thankful, appreciation truly validates. Of course, recognition that takes place in front of others amplifies the effect. People stand taller; they want to do more, and they certainly want to be around someone who values both their contribution and them as people. I try to do that in my office, and I can see the amazing impact that it has on our team.

We Need Each Other

Once I had mastered the wisdom behind my father's philosophy - just be - I came to another life-changing realization. As a result of beginning to love and accept myself, I found it even easier to love and accept others without them having to do anything to make it happen.

The truth is that we need other people in order to enable us to fulfill our life goals. They are your leverage; you simply cannot maximize your potential without them. You have a role to play, but you have to allow others to play their role, too. Possibility-thinking opens the door to many opportunities that require teamwork. If you want to maximize your success, you will need to partner with other people. And then it is all about everyone. When you start to do truly great things, it can no longer be just about you. That is invaluable. There is no limit to what you can achieve in life, together.

Recognizing the Good in Every Part of Life

"Enjoy the little things, for one day you may look back and realize they were the big things."
- Robert Brault

I love to go walking at night with my daughter, it's something we've done since she was when she was 6 years old. She has always loved those walks. We still occasionally get the chance to take one at the end of the day just as everyone is winding down for the night. We leave our cell phones behind so no one can interrupt "our time." For the first one hundred yards or so, we just take in the silence of the evening. Pretty soon, we start a conversation about what was happening in our lives. Sometimes I throw out a quote from a book I'm reading, or one I've heard on a tape, and she tells me what she thinks of it. We always finish our walks with what has become a tradition: "What two things

Jose and April Feliciano

are you proud of today?" It takes more thoughtfulness to think about the good things that happened in our day than to simply blurt out the bad stuff, which doesn't make us feel good anyway.

One of the things I am proud of every day is my family. Popular culture suggests that busy fathers and their daughters cannot be close. I have read sad statistics about how many fathers only spend an average of seven minutes a day talking to and interacting with their children. Apparently, teens and parents are not supposed to get along. Current thinking implies that being estranged from our kids when they are teens is normal.

It is as inaccurate as saying, "Every boss is difficult," or "After twenty years of marriage, you cannot expect to be in love anymore," or "Older parents are a burden on their children." I figured out a long time ago that these statements are often excuses for not putting effort into our relationships.

While I don't expect things from people, I expect myself to find the best in them. I look for the good in every person I love as if I were searching for treasure, and I celebrate all that I discover.

Do We Forget to Celebrate the Status Quo?

It seems to me that as we move forward in our lives, we often forget to celebrate the steps that got us there, and we even forget to celebrate each key point of arrival. Thanks to a few bumps in the road that scared me, I found a jewel in life that I love to celebrate: that beautiful word called "normal". When I look at many other people's "normal", I am reminded every day to be grateful for my own. What we consider "poor" in this country would represent wealth in other countries; for example, most homes have a TV, a microwave, a dishwasher, a car, a DVD player, a computer and cable television, along with fast food a couple of times a week. This is unheard of in a large number of countries around the world, such as Africa, China, Central America and India.

The next thing I have learned to celebrate humbly and gratefully is my own achievements. When you begin to understand your full potential and look at what you are doing each day to actually fulfill it, being the best version of yourself takes on a whole new meaning. It can be a lesson in humility or a kick in the pants. I never forget whose hand is at my back, and I never forget to say thank you or to celebrate.

It is a way of honoring the source of the lessons and gifts received, and celebration is simply an expression of appreciation.

I am still learning that it is okay to want to be, do, and have more in life. We are taught from a young age not to be greedy. That is like telling a child in a candy store, "Don't touch and don't taste!" The opposite is important. The more we envision for ourselves, the more likely we are to do good things around us, simply as a byproduct of reaching for our own dreams. Aspiration breeds imagination and leads to innovation.

I once helped a colleague of mine put some of her future goals down on paper so she could begin mapping out some realistic steps to get there. Her dream included a certain standard of living and driving a certain type of car. Later, she shared her list with a friend who made the offhanded comment that her list seemed "greedy." This hurt my colleague immensely and she began to question the validity of her goals.

We have to learn to live without worrying about what other people think. There is a sense of freedom when you begin to celebrate life on your own terms. You can either live in heaven or hell in your own mind; you can be miserable trying to live up to the standards of others, or you can just be and do the best that you can and experience a little bit of heaven on earth.

We limit ourselves when we let others dictate what and when we should celebrate. Sometimes, we are our own worst enemy.

Sometimes Life is About Losing and Then Winning

If one of the keys to having more in life is celebrating all the good things, then we must be able to hold onto

those good things even when we experience difficulty or disappointment. Sometimes, there can be hidden benefits in failure, if we know where to look for them.

My little league team had a perfect record season after season.

No one scored a touchdown against us, and the kids were proud of their perfect record. Then, a team from Dallas came to town; these guys were the biggest grade school kids I had ever seen in my life, and they mowed my little guys down like weeds within the first five minutes of the game. It was difficult to deal with losing when they were used to winning all the time; we had a roster full of skinny, scrappy, and scrawny players, but we were the smartest team by far. I had always reminded them, "Smart beats strong."

I stood there clenching my jaw as they limped over to the sidelines. They unsnapped their helmets and, before I knew it, I had eleven little boys all bawling on the bench. I drew a deep breath and said, "Boys, we all knew that this would be a challenge. We're stepping into the big leagues, and we have to expect a few bruises along the way. I am proud of us because we are tackling something bigger than ourselves. Part of winning is growing and being challenged." With that, I clapped my hands, slapped some shoulder pads, and sent them onto the field. Our opponents scored on us again in the next series of plays.

We ended up with our first loss in three years, but none of us were defeated. We had all just taken on a giant for the first time, so we were elated. This happened two weeks before they would enter junior high.

I already knew how challenging it was going to be for these kids without the added pressure of their self-confidence being at stake. Now, however, they knew they could take on giants and challenges.

The parents were more frustrated than the kids, who "got it." The kids and I ate pizza and celebrated our success in meeting the challenge. Many of those kids played on both the T.K. Gorman High School and John Tyler High School championship teams as seniors.

I am convinced that my guys learned something more valuable than a win on the scoreboard. They learned that sometimes winning all of your games is not as important as how you view the losses.

Finding something good in every situation means being open to what you can learn through difficulty. If you are open to learning, even the tough times can be beneficial. Winston Churchill, who triumphed over the Nazi regime in WWII, had some wise advice about overcoming adversity. He said, "If you're going through hell, keep going."

Don't RSVP to A Pity Party

When we face trials, it can be tempting to throw a pity party in honor of all the things that are going wrong in our lives, rather than to recognize all that is going well. I like this poem about self pity by Jessica Nelson North:

I had a little tea party, This afternoon at three;
'Twas very small, Three guests in all,
Just I, myself, and me.
Myself ate up the sandwiches, While I drank all the tea,
'Twas also I who ate the pie
and passed the cake to me.

You may receive an invitation to a pity party in your honor, but do not RSVP!

One thing we have in our family is a lot of love; it doesn't matter how much money someone has or does not have. Sure, there were times when we were tempted to feel depressed or sorry for ourselves, but that never lasted long.

Together, we made it through when we had to scramble to come up with fifty dollars for rent. The air was blowing through the walls of our home, but the nucleus of each of these experiences was the love we have for each other, and you can't put a price tag on that. Instead of feeling sorry for the tough times we've been through, we look back and see all of the good that happened despite it all, and that's worth celebrating. Albert Einstein wisely said, "There are only two ways to live your life: one is as though nothing is a miracle, and the other is as though everything is a miracle."

Oh, the Places We've Been!

One of the exercises I like our office to do at the start of a new year is to write down everything we accomplished the previous year so that we can reflect on a job well done. Goal-setting is crucial, as it creates measurable milestones for success.

Showing what a business or family has accomplished together is like a treasure map. It shows all the places we have been and where we are headed next. Sometimes we look ahead to the next year, forgetting to give credit to the past year for all the lessons and gifts it has given us. You may not have, do, or be all that you want just yet, but take special note of all you have accomplished in your life thus far, and head for the future with the fuel of past successes driving you forward. A family or business that regularly takes time to celebrate their accomplishments and the impact they have had on others is more likely to stay successful.

Do you ever get the feeling that you are not progressing quickly enough? Taking the time to celebrate milestones on your journey to success can give you a better sense of how far you have come, as well as help you decide which direction to take next.

Be Part of Something Grand

Is the vision you have created for your life worth celebrating? Is it something so outrageous that, if and when it happens, you will feel like throwing a huge party? Think back with me to the story of the Two-Hour House. What inspired those people to dedicate several years of their lives to something that everyone was telling them couldn't be done? They wanted to be part of something grand; people want to be part of something special.

People in a family, business, or team get excited once they understand that the direction being taken will allow them to be part of something much bigger than themselves. It's like being invited to be part of something magical. Our book, *2 Hour House*, shares a story about one of the volunteers who felt like they were part of something extraordinary.

I'll never forget the story Dick Schilhab told about one of the concrete truck drivers who later moved to another town. The manager from the trucking company in the new town called Dick one day as a routine check on the driver's references. In the course of the conversation, the manager let Dick know an interesting thing about the driver's application.

On his application, the driver had written "I drove for the Two-Hour House". Tell that man that his job, although brief, was still important that day. His pride and ownership during the event was a result of raising expectations for everyone who participated. For him to say he drove for the Two-Hour House meant something more to him than just filling in blanks on an application.

Celebrating being part of something grand creates a culture where people feel connected to something larger than themselves. When we start identifying all the ways we are making a difference in the world, we create a cause for celebration, and then even the smallest things we do take on new meaning. Albert Giacometti, a sculptor, came to this realization when he said, "Basically, I no longer work for anything but the sensation I have while working." That is finding true joy in one's work and life—no hidden agendas, no manipulating others, no thought of what's in it for me— just pure exhilaration.

Little Things Mean A Lot

As the guardian of my siblings, I understood the importance of attending their school and sporting events. I wanted to make sure that they always knew someone cared enough to celebrate and support their goals.

One time, I drove two and a half hours one way just to watch my sister's five-minute swim race, simply because I wanted Juanita to know that I was there to support her. I only missed one of my brother Jeff's games throughout his entire high school basketball and baseball career. We still talk about it, as he hit the final shot and won the game; it was even on the front page of the sports section of the local newspaper. Just my luck!

Celebrate Others

One of the greatest gifts we can give to someone else is encouragement when they are too tired or busy to see anything noteworthy in themselves or their situation. Sometimes, we just need to let them look through our eyes and see themselves from a different perspective.

I have a Character First card that I always keep in my wallet. At our company's Christmas party one year, I listed every employee in our firm and associated each one with a particular character trait I saw in their lives at work. I thought of words like *honorable, hospitable, dependable,* and *trustworthy.*

When I came to the word "flexibility," I named two or three people and explained how I saw that trait at work in their lives. I then came to the word "forgiveness" and named two or three others.

I noticed that even when it was not someone's turn to be honored, each person was looking around, smiling at each other and nodding. It was as if they were acknowledging, "Yes, I see that trait at work in that person too." Suddenly, we all realized we were part of a very special group of people - people who were sincere, unusually thoughtful, tolerant, and responsible.

The atmosphere in the room lit up with a sense of pride we felt toward one another, causing a cause for celebration. We all realized that we had the best people on the planet working together toward something significant, making us all want to be a part of it.

Thrive of Encouragement

My mother is the greatest example of finding the good in every situation. In my family, I am surrounded by people who are positive thinkers and who are open to all kinds of possibilities.

If you have big dreams and goals ahead of you, do yourself a favor and seek out others with the same philosophy and approach to life.

I call them "the people who motivate"; be on the lookout for similar souls who share your belief that everything is possible.

Trusting Others and Doing More Together

"Trust is the glue of life. It's the most essential ingredient in effective communication. It's the foundational principle that holds all relationships."
- Stephen Covey

To return once again to the analogy of the runner preparing to run a marathon, the question is not only, "What will you do to get ready to run your 26 miles?" but also "What will you need to stop doing in order to achieve it?"

If you don't understand this important principle, you may feel overwhelmed by the idea of making changes as you will view it as adding a whole new set of activities and responsibilities to your already busy life. When will you find the time? How will you balance it with your other responsibilities? Instead of making your life easier, more efficient, and more effective, you will perceive the possibilities as a burden, not a blessing.

Refining Your To-Do List

With the marathon in mind, let's say that you decide to start by running two miles three to five times a week. You work a full day from home or at the office, arrange dinner, get your children to soccer practice, pick up around the house or yard, help the kids with their homework until bedtime, and then crash into bed yourself - only to wake up and do the same thing all over again tomorrow.

Without making any adjustments to your already crammed schedule, you will be frazzled and frustrated by the end of the first week! Instead, you must make room for a new and positive lifestyle. We often think of delegating as a principle related to tasks at the office, but it should apply to many areas of our lives.

What could you stop doing (tasks that can be delegated) that would make room in your life for something you want to *start* doing? Maybe you spend an hour a week taking your kids back and forth to soccer practice; join a carpool with other soccer moms. Delegate some household chores to family members to free up an extra forty-five minutes to an hour. Create or join a supper club and delegate a meal or two each week among a group of friends.

We must curb the impulse to do everything ourselves if we want to create space for our goals. The power of delegation is amazing when used properly.

Your Quality of Life Matters

There are some things in our lives that we must delegate and some things that we simply have to do ourselves. You can delegate your tax preparation to an expert, but you can't delegate a Saturday morning aerobics class to someone else to do for you just so that you can check it off your list. Likewise, you can't delegate the practice of your personal faith or religion. And you cannot delegate fun. (If you could, I'd say to delegate it to me and I'll have all the fun possible for both of us!) However, there are things that you *can* and should delegate if you want to reach your goals.

I worked with a client who was passionate about coffee and had a strong desire to spend more time with her children. She was a professional career woman, trying to balance the responsibilities of being a mother and managing the household. After working a full week, she would clean the house on Saturday mornings, doing laundry and other chores that she could not complete during the week.

However, what she most wanted to do on Saturday mornings was to spend quality time with her boys. We have a tool we use in my practice called a Quality of Life Enhancer. It basically asks people to complete an exercise to help them identify what would increase the quality of their lives.

Once she had completed the exercise, she began to see a disparity between what was most important to her (her values) and how she was actually spending her time. She realized that spending more time with her children would reflect her values and improve her quality of life. However, she felt as though her time was not her own, and she told herself that she could not delegate the household chores to someone else because she could not afford the extra $100 out of the family budget. She felt torn.

It was clear that spending as much time as possible with her family was the number one goal in her life, which aligned with her personal values. I asked what it would take to achieve this. She had been envisioning the $100 as an additional expense, but I suggested to her that she make her coffee at home instead of going to the coffee shop every day. This eliminated the expense. This is an example of prioritizing. The reward of her adjustment would be gaining several hours a week with her boys.

So many times we live like this single mom did, feeling like what we want out of life is unattainable and impossible. Just the opposite of possibility-thinking, we run out of hope when we run out of possibilities. We have to do something radical to break out of that thought pattern; fortunately, my client did and it revolutionized her home life.

She realized that she could not delegate time with her boys to someone else; no one else could replace her sitting beside them at the breakfast table talking. However, she could delegate the housework, and she did. What seemed

like a sacrifice at first reaped more dividends than she could
have imagined.

It is possible to experience more happiness and fulfillment in our lives and in our families if we learn to prioritize.
There will always be much more that needs to be done than
we can do ourselves; we have to learn to distinguish between
what only we can do and what should be passed on to others.

Fact or Fiction

To learn how to delegate tasks and responsibilities and
increase our quality of life, we need to get serious about
certain false beliefs or misconceptions we have bought into.
We all have misunderstandings surrounding the concept of
delegating; otherwise, we would do it more often.

Misconception: "I'm the only one who can do what I do."
Truth: Look around carefully; if you weren't there,
someone else could take on the task.

I have seen people accept all the responsibility for a task
because they are convinced that there is no one else to do
it. In fact, this belief is so strong that they never even ask
if someone else can or will help! This happens in organizations, and I have seen it occur in families as well.

In families, it may look something like this: Parents reach
a certain age where they need help taking care of themselves.
Bob sees that his parents need increased care, so he assumes
full responsibility for the task at hand. At first, he feels
needed and important as the sole caregiver. As the eldest,
he had always assumed this responsibility would fall to him
anyway, although this has never been discussed among the

siblings; this is just Bob's assumption.

Over time, however, he feels pressured by the increasing time commitment of driving his parents to medical appointments and keeping all their medication straight. He had no idea it would be so exhausting. The parents feel guilty, but Bob assures them that it is fine.

Only it's not.

Soon, he begins to envy his siblings' lifestyle; footloose and fancy free while he is "doing all the work" caring for their parents. Every time his sister sends photos from their most recent Cancun family vacation, he feels resentful. He starts to feel like someone owes him something, but he has never asked for help from his siblings, nor has he let them know how much of a burden it is on his own family. The siblings are pleased that their parents seem to be doing so well and never give Bob's silent anguish a second thought.

Eventually, his resentment boiled over. Suddenly, there was a family rift between the siblings that no one, except Bob, had ever seen coming.

The dynamic here is quite simple. Oftentimes, we unintentionally put ourselves in positions of stress and anxiety because we do not ask for help. We observe what needs to be done and take it upon ourselves to do it. Those who have not learned the power of delegation keep the problem and solution in their own hands. They do not realize that a major reason for their anger and resentment is their own unwillingness to share the load - to delegate. All of their energy is directed toward everything that they are doing alone, instead of taking advantage of opportunities to share the burden. This is a volatile recipe for ruined relationships.

When an organization is led along similar lines, it is the same story, just a different verse. Whether we are the president of an organization or head of our department and we do not delegate properly or set clear expectations, things soon begin to break down.

Our natural inclination is to take back all of the responsibility and do it all ourselves. In doing so, we make the situation worse by failing to recognize the very thing that caused the disaster: our inability to delegate! Leo Tolstoy once observed, "Everyone thinks of changing the world, but no one thinks of changing himself."

In some ways, large or small, we contribute to the effect in everything. If we experience a great outcome in a certain situation, we know that we did something positive that contributed to the effect of that outcome. If it is a negative outcome, we should also look inside first, not look for someone else to blame.

Most disappointments can be traced to one of a few causes: either we

1. *Give others a task that they're not qualified to do, or;*
2. *They don't accept the responsibility or;*
3. *Our definition of the expectations is unclear.*

Will Rogers said, "If you never want to be disappointed, don't expect too much." People who don't delegate often end up doing everything themselves in order to avoid being disappointed. Some people are afraid to delegate in case they lose control and appear to be at fault. They delegate as little as possible and exhaust themselves, even though others are willing to help. Once we start to adopt this mentality, we're in trouble.

In families, relationships can suffer. In companies, the bottom line can suffer. Delegating can give you more time, energy, and resources to accomplish the things on your list that are both important and for which you are gifted.

Don't try to tell this to those who refuse to delegate; they are firmly convinced that taking their hands off a project will harm the end goal. On the other hand, things could go better if they would learn to communicate and delegate.

Misconception: No one else wants the responsibilities I handle.
Truth: People like rising to new challenges, as long as they understand the expectations.

How will you know what talents your team has unless you are willing to give them new opportunities? Highly motivated people are lifelong learners; they are interested in every aspect of their company, including other roles not necessarily related to their primary job. A company may have their best salesperson right under their nose, only presently misplaced as the new receptionist who is eager to get into sales.

Delegating is an excellent way to discover hidden talent. Hoarding responsibilities impedes everyone's growth. You cannot honestly say, "No one wants my responsibilities" until you have clearly articulated what you are doing and offered someone else an opportunity to attempt it. Communicate your needs, set the expectations, and unleash the potential talent.

I have noticed that any time I have a new hire, they are always better than the person I had before. Why is that? Is the job changing? No, the general responsibilities remain much the same. Are better people coming to my door? Maybe. I would rather think that it has more to do with the fact that I am learning how to be a better employer by setting clear expectations.

With every hire, I gain more knowledge of what I want, making it easier for a new person to deliver the desired results.

"I'm the one who has to do everything. Nobody around here wants to do the dirty work," muttered the mother as she picked up the dirty socks and wet towels off the bathroom floor for the thirty-seventh time that week and stuffed another sock into the laundry hamper. You can see how this relates to families.

It is so tempting to play the role of the martyr and take it all on ourselves, when all we have to do is explain the family expectations in a way that everyone understands their part. What if she went to her husband and children, sat them down on the couch, and together they laid out a new plan where everyone became responsible for doing a portion of the family laundry?

There are certain things that you are especially gifted at accomplishing. These are the things that you can and should be doing. However, there are just as many tasks and responsibilities that may be important, but for which you have no gift or time. If you learn how to delegate what drains you emotionally and physically, you will increase your effectiveness tenfold.

Still think nobody wants your responsibilities? How do you know until you ask? Keeping the show running doesn't have to mean you're running the show.

Misconception: "I have to do everything myself if I want it done right."
Truth: Others can do it as well as you can. Sometimes even better

If you are convinced that no one can perform a responsibility or contribute to an idea as well as you can, you might question your leadership skills. This applies to employers and team leaders who are accountable for the personal and professional development of their team, as well as to parents whose main job is to grow their children into responsible adults.

Part of what determines our approach to delegating to other people are our beliefs about them, which form our expectations. The same goes for our children. If we believe we have smart, talented children, we will expect more out of them and give them tasks that challenge their potential. And guess what happens with children whose parents believe they are smart, talented, and responsible? They usually turn out to be exactly that. Children, like our other relationships, rise to meet our expectations of them.

No man goes to work and says to himself, "I hope I get to mess something up today?" No child thinks, "I hope I do something today to disappoint my parents?" Deep down, everyone longs to do an extraordinary job and belong. We just have to draw it out of them.

My maternal grandfather used to always say positive things about us as kids. He would give out compliments and encouragement as if he were handing out fistfuls of candy.

"They're smart boys," he would say about my brother John and me. "You're going to do something with your life." He spoke so highly of so many positive things in our lives. No wonder we loved having him around. Someone else's confidence in you can change your life. Your confidence in someone else can change theirs!

Of course, there are those who don't seem to believe that other people are gifted with intelligence beyond the average. We know this by the way they hoard the most important tasks and responsibilities. Then, a sad thing happens; after a while, the people closest to them begin to doubt their own abilities. Their minds and talents atrophy, like muscles they never get to use.

We need more people at work and at home like my grandfather who can entice the best out of others by simply tuning into their "can-do" side. If you want to enhance your team's skills, don't take away important tasks; demonstrate confidence in them by giving them more. Increase your child's self-esteem by entrusting them with responsibilities around the house. Your confidence in others can amplify their skills in dramatic ways.

There is a specific way to demonstrate confidence in others when giving them a task: clarify the outcome you desire and then step away from their process.

In my office, one of the main objectives for my team is to make clients feel loved and appreciated. I cannot tell my team exactly how to do it or it will appear insincere. If I have done my job correctly, I will have ten different employees ensuring clients feel the love in ten different ways. Each team member will use their individual talents to achieve this. Conventional wisdom suggests that one should build a step-by-step process that everyone could follow. However, smart delegation requires me to explain the desired outcome and then allow them to find their own ways to accomplish it. Not everyone's personality can fit into one process as everyone is different.

A single person tackling a project can come up with one scenario, but two or three people can create what I like to think of as a *mastermind group*, able to churn out ideas and solutions at a faster rate and of better quality. This is called synergy, as it plays to everyone's strengths, wisdom, and experience. While you are free to do everything yourself, don't think that this is the only way it can be done correctly; it will simply be done the way you think is right.

If you have doubts about the power of delegation, take an extended vacation and find out what gets done without you being around.

There is a large, old cemetery in the middle of the city where I live. On either side are heavily trafficked streets filled with everyday activities. The gravestones bear the names of many people who were convinced that life would fall apart and grind to a halt if they did not do whatever it was they used to do. It is a sober reminder of feeling absolutely irreplaceable.

Learning to Delegate As a Matter of Trust

It all comes down to a matter of trust. At the office, if a major project needs to be completed we'll either trust someone else to get it done - or we won't. At home, we'll either trust our spouse to help run the household or we won't.

Spouses often go back and undo what the other has done to resolve an issue. Imagine "Joey," a typical teenage boy, breaking curfew for the second time in a week. His father goes to Joey and grounds him for a week. "I wouldn't have done it that way," the wife thinks when she finds out what happened. She marches back into Joey's room and lifts the sentence that the father just imposed. Joey is thrilled, but the father feels frustrated and powerless. Trust has been violated.

Our level of trust indicates whether we are operating primarily out of fear *("Oh no! Someone else will mess it up if I let them do it")* or if we are learning to empower people by delegating *("Great! I believe someone else can do an even better job than I can")*.

One of the highest compliments a client can give me is to hand me a hard-earned dollar. They are saying, "I trust you to manage this for me." I have never lost sight of that privilege. Nevertheless, I have also learned that if you want people to trust you, you must first be willing to demonstrate trust. I understand that a lot of people come to the point where it is hard to trust others to help them. However, I have always believed that if one person out of a hundred burns you, it does not mean that the other ninety-nine will follow suit.

The alternative is not to trust anyone, convinced that someone is out to get you. Imagine two wealthy children playing kickball in the street with less affluent kids nearby. The wealthy father says, "Don't play with them," creating a barrier. By instilling that small seed of mistrust and division in the heart of a child, they will grow up not knowing who

to trust. It is a horrible thing to do. Still, many people, especially those who have been burned, think that others have to
earn their trust first.

Trust people from the outset until they "un-earn" it. This
may go against conventional wisdom, but most people will
reciprocate. You will have a better relationship if you start
with trust rather than waiting for it to come in slowly.

Where Are You Focused

Consider the myriad of opportunities we gain when we
shift our focus from the one in a hundred people who will
disappoint us to the ninety-nine we can trust enough to
share responsibilities and build our dreams together.

Possibilities shrink when you focus on what is wrong
with a person, situation, or circumstance. Possibility-thinking focuses on what is good and asks, "How can I make it
better?" Learning to improve and optimize who you are,
what you do, and what you have is fundamental to possibility
thinking.

Communications

*"The single biggest problem with communication is the
illusion that it has taken place."*
- George Bernard Shaw

I have always believed that sustained success almost
invariably comes down to the relationships we are able
to build and maintain in both our business and personal
lives. Relationships, both good and bad, are influenced by
our ability to communicate. Whether we are talking about
our clients, the people we work for, the people who work for
us, or even our family and friends -- long-lasting happiness
and success, most of the time, is a direct result of the impact
we have on others and they have on us.

It might seem simple, but it is really the little things that
have a positive impact which builds and nurtures the direction of our lives. And here is the thing: this is nothing new.
The concept of building and maintaining relationships, and
communicating effectively, is as old as business itself. Fifty
years ago, we would not have been talking about it; it was

just the way things were done.

Technology has made communication easier, but in the process, we have lost the individual, personal contact we had with our clients. Nowadays, we can email, text, and tweet at will, but we are not connecting. We can reach the top on our own, but it may not be as rewarding or enjoyable. Relationships are based on shared experiences; for example, a movie is more enjoyable in a big theater with other people than when watching it alone at home.

The book *The Secret*, among many other self-improvement books, explains how to get what we want. It emphasizes that our focus determines our outcome, which is a recurring theme. Our ability to communicate our thoughts, goals, and processes more effectively is what makes the real difference. Great communication takes a little more effort and tends to be collaborative, with clearly defined goals and expectations. It is often referred to as Common Goal Communication and probably offers the most effective and sustainable successes.

Family dynasties, Fortune 500 companies, sporting achievements, Mount Rushmore, and incredible architecture are all examples of great common goal communication, and they all require strong leadership, a clear vision, and great collaboration around a central idea, much like a symphony orchestra and its conductor. With all other elements of an orchestra being equal, it is the conductor - the leader, the communicator - that really makes the difference between a good and a great orchestra.

In our orchestra, the musicians all have the same level of talent; they can all read and play the music, follow the pauses

and rhythms. The sheet music for a specific composition is identical, so everyone is literally on the same page. Orchestras are grouped into teams, or what they call sections, and unless you're playing a Stradivarius, the instruments have similar tones, creating the same musical notes and flavors. Given all these conceits, what sets the best orchestras apart? Well, some orchestras are able to rehearse more than others; some concert seasons are longer than others, and the members of the orchestra have the opportunity to work together more, allowing them to recognize each other's strengths and weaknesses and maximize their strengths by learning from each other. Some instruments are better than others, true, but in the wrong hands a Stradivarius can sound like a Wal-Mart special. Likewise, even a simple instrument can sound wonderful in the hands of an expert performer.

And, as within any organization, individual musicians bring different life experiences that color or shade the music they play. To a certain extent, then, it can be argued that the most important variable in every orchestra is the passion and experience of their conductor. It all begins with the conductor's ability and desire to communicate their vision and interpretation of the piece to every member of their orchestra with clarity, belief, and passion.

Some conductors have a more intimate knowledge of a particular piece: its history, its level of difficulty, its mood, and sometimes its intention - realizing the *1812 Overture* is a triumphant celebration of a victory. Great conductors know exactly what they want to hear and the emotions or feelings they want a particular piece of music to communicate. They have the ability to better tone, infuse, and communicate their passion to every member of the orchestra in such a way that the orchestra is inspired and able to understand and deliver what is being asked of them.

We are all only as good as the company we keep. To that end, a good musician becomes a better musician under the direction of a great conductor. A good employee becomes a better employee under the direction of great management. In business, when there is a common vision and passion, 'chemistry' occurs. Limits and individual goals are abandoned in favor of something potentially greater, and most of us want to be part of something that changes us in a profound way forever. When a good leader shares their interpretation or vision for a project with passion and believability, and it touches us, it makes us all want to be part of that vision.

Symbols

"The world is full of magic things, patiently waiting
for our senses to grow sharper."
- W.B. Yeats

Words and symbols are interpretive. Take a look around the room you're sitting in and make a mental note of what you see. Based on our life experiences, each of us sees this room a little differently. We have a tendency to focus on what we know, on what we have learned over the years to pay attention to, and to concentrate on what is important to us.

We are all looking at the same room; the same walls, rug, lights, chairs, and the same people. Those of us who have recently shopped for a rug might be focusing more on the rug - its color, pattern, and texture, or how much it cost per square foot.

Our focus in life is experiential. A few years back, I was rear-ended while waiting at a stoplight. The other car didn't realize the light was red, and was going 35 miles an hour when they hit me. I never saw them coming. For the next year or so, every time I was waiting at a stoplight, my eyes would keep looking in the rear-view mirror to see if someone was going to hit me. Our focus is experiential, and being rear-ended changed my driving habits.

In all my years of driving, I had never been rear-ended before I was rear-ended, and have never been rear-ended since. But that experience, for the longest time, made me distrust the driving ability of virtually everyone that was behind me at a stoplight.

What we see, and how we react to what we see, how we respond emotionally, is because of our unique life experiences. Which I hope serves to illustrate that our experiences also dictate how we sell, how we approach a simple discussion, how we resolve disputes, and how we react to the world around us. There is no right or wrong, no black and white in this game, just a thousand shades of gray. And as professionals, we need to realize what we say isn't always heard and understood the way it was intended. And, as importantly, what we hear isn't always what's being said.

And just like being rear-ended, any random event, or even a simple suggestion, can change our perception of the world.

Take another quick look around the room and remember the first thing that comes to your mind.

Did you focus on the rug I talked about earlier? Or about that last time you had a close call in your car after I told you about being rear-ended? Because we all make connections through our own filter. If you weren't thinking about the rug or being rear-ended, what were you thinking about? And why?

When I mentioned the rug, were you thinking about the last time you bought one, or about lunch, or your children, or the business meeting you have scheduled for next week, or how much longer this bald guy was going to be talking?

Now, I want you to look around the room again, but before you do, think of the color red. Look around the room concentrating on the color red.

Now, look again, but this time the color is blue.

The room hasn't changed, just our focus on those colors - because the simple mention of a color opened our eyes to what was always right in front of us.

The way we perceive a room can change dramatically depending on the color we focus on. When we are told to concentrate on a particular color, our brains tend to filter out other colors and focus on the one that was mentioned. This can make the room look completely different from when we focus on a different color.

For example, if someone is told to concentrate on the color red in a room, their attention is drawn to objects or surfaces that are predominantly red. The red may appear more intense and dominant than it actually is, making the room feel warmer and more energetic. On the other hand, if someone is told to concentrate on the color blue, their attention will be drawn to blue objects or surfaces, and the room may appear cooler and more calming.

Moreover, if someone is asked to shift their focus to a different color, it can change their perception of the room once again. For instance, if someone is asked to focus on the color green after focusing on red, they may notice green objects that were not noticeable before. The room may then appear more balanced and harmonious, with a sense of nature and growth.

In this way, the suggestion of a particular color can alter our perception of a room, and shifting our focus to a different color can change that perception once again.

People's perceptions are constantly shaped and influenced by their experiences. Our experiences, both positive and negative, shape the way we view the world and the people in it. Whether we realize it or not, our experiences impact our beliefs, attitudes, and values, leading to shifts in our perceptions over time.

Positive experiences can broaden our perceptions, leading us to be more open-minded and accepting. For example, traveling to a new place and experiencing a different culture can broaden our understanding and appreciation for different ways of life. Similarly, positive interactions with people from diverse backgrounds can challenge our preconceptions and biases, leading to more inclusive and tolerant attitudes.

On the other hand, negative experiences can narrow our perceptions, leading us to be more closed-minded and skeptical. Traumatic events, for instance, can lead to feelings of fear and distrust, causing individuals to view the world as a dangerous and hostile place.

Moreover, our perceptions can change based on the intensity and frequency of our experiences. Repeated positive experiences can reinforce our positive perceptions, while repeated negative experiences can reinforce negative perceptions.

This makes me wonder how much opportunity is staring us in the face every day that we just don't see. As professionals, we need to be able to sit back and take in the world around us, be open to new ideas, and to the opportunities that are right in front of our eyes. We need to be open and to always take a second look around the room by changing our focus.

It's the difference between the narrow thinking of "should be" and being open to the possibilities of "could be." Before we talked about the red or blue, most of us didn't focus on the colors in the room. If we didn't see the colors, what else are we missing?

When dealing with prospects, clients, or even our co-workers, we need to practice empathy, which is simply the ability to recognize and share the feelings that are being experienced by others. It is conscious and the cornerstone in genuine human relationships.

Empathy not only makes us better people, but is the key to being better at what we do for a living, allowing us to consistently switch our focus and see all the opportunities around us.

Being a Lifelong Learner and Asking Questions

"The capacity to learn is a gift; the ability to learn is a skill; the willingness to learn is a choice."
- Brian Herbert

What prevents us from asking questions and exploring possibilities? When should we decide it is no longer safe to explore the world around us and adopt the approach of being a lifelong learner?

I think it begins when we are young. At some point in our lives, our questions are challenged in a negative manner and we suddenly feel diminished. Someone may tell us that we should already know better, or we may be told that we should already know it all. I am not sure when this "already" is. It is as if we cross some imaginary line where we think we must either appear to be experts on all topics or we are a fool for having to ask questions.

When we stop asking questions, we start filling in the

blanks by assuming what we don't know. When my daughter was in sixth grade, her teacher told the class, "Don't ask a foolish question." Well, what is a foolish question? Nobody knew! The students weren't sure if their question met the teacher's criteria for foolishness or not - so guess what? No one asked any questions that semester, and I am willing to bet that no one learned very much either. Right there, a whole classroom learned that being silent was safer.

The only foolish question is the one that we are afraid to ask. No genuine question is foolish. Only by asking questions can we reach the goals we desire.

Socrates was one of the greatest educators. He taught by asking questions; this is known as the Socratic Method. He drew out the answers from his pupils, which is the root meaning of the word "education" (duco, meaning "to draw out"). Socrates would grill his students with non-stop questions about specific subjects, making it a safe environment for learning.

His questions encouraged them to ask more questions in order to increase their knowledge. What would happen if we implemented this same style of comprehensive, 360-degree thinking today in order to move ourselves and others towards their goals and not away from them?

It happens to all of us. My wife's story is similar. One day at the beginning of the semester of her ninth-grade Algebra class, the teacher (who was also a coach) introduced the class to variables. With a room full of wide-eyed freshmen in their first week of high school, I imagine that the x and y variables in the equations were not the only unknowns that day. These guys and gals had questions - and lots of them -

but everyone was too shy to raise their hands and interrupt the big, burly man at the front.

Finally, one of the football players asked a question only to be totally humiliated in front of the entire class. My wife said that from that day forward she never asked the teacher a question out of fear of public humiliation.

The truth is that we stop learning when we stop asking questions. We will never reach our fullest potential if we don't ask questions that move us closer to our goals. The more facts we have about a situation or idea, the better equipped we are to make wiser decisions.

The alternative is to pretend that we know something that we do not. Instead of being motivated to find out the answers, we learn to fake it in order to remain safe. Instead of being lifelong learners, we cheat ourselves out of the opportunity to truly know, rather than assuming; and assuming can be a very dangerous thing.

Just Readin' It Ain't Gettin It

Several years ago, I was speaking to a large group of financial advisors. I love asking questions, so I asked this group of successful men and women, how many of them had read Steven Covey's book, The Seven Habits of Highly Effective People? About half of the people in the room eagerly raised their hands. Then I asked, "How many of you can recite all seven habits?" Not a single person could.

We can read material without internalizing it; we may love it and agree with it, but we don't really know it. For example, we cannot practice the habits of effective people if we have not internalized them.

It's like telling a good joke; when I hear one, I have to practice it several times before I can tell it easily enough to make others laugh. It's the same with learning; if I haven't internalized it, I know I won't practice it.

There is an old proverb that states, "What we don't know can't hurt us." However, this is incorrect; what you don't know can hurt you. I heard a story about a man who rushed into a pharmacy and exclaimed to the pharmacist, "Quickly! I need something to stop my hiccups!" The man then quickly ran down an aisle in the store, searching for a product to help.

As he searched the shelves, the pharmacist snuck up behind him and hit him with a karate chop to the neck, yelling, "Boo!" The startled man looked up from the floor, rubbing his neck and asked, "What on earth did you do that for?"

The pharmacist smiled and said, "Well, I bet you don't have the hiccups anymore." The man replied, "I never did! It's my wife out in the car who has the hiccups!" They say that what we don't know can hurt us!

As a business owner, I may assume that I know the best way to handle a dispute among employees without asking any questions. However, how much more effective would my resolution be if I took the time to ask enough questions and identify the real problem? When we don't ask questions, we start to fill in the blanks from a limited source of knowledge and make assumptions that may be totally incorrect and, worse, detrimental.

What could have been a weakness in our family system has instead become a great strength. I am not afraid to ask questions or admit when I don't know something; I'm

always quick to say, "I know that I don't know!" When I became the guardian of my brothers and sister, I didn't pretend to automatically know what to do; instead, I read a lot and asked a lot of questions. I found people more than ready to help me with the challenges I encountered along the way; I just had to ask. Learning to ask is like having gold nuggets in your pocket.

Mentoring

I believe mentoring is the quickest way to progress in any aspect of life - our work, our faith, our health. Mentoring is mainly a relationship between a mentor and mentee. As we mature, we learn that when the mentee is prepared, the mentor will appear.

Mentoring Thrives On Curiosity. When a child is old enough to talk, one of their favorite words is "why?" They ask, "Why is the sky blue? Why is the grass green?" Children are naturally curious about how the world works, and parents are natural mentors to them.

Our kids can drive us crazy sometimes with all the "why's" of life, but every question presents us with a teachable moment. Saying, "I'm glad you asked" reinforces their willingness to learn what they don't know. We have to train children to ask questions to speed up and enhance their mental growth.

Another lesson I learned in a parenting class called "Growing Kids God's Way" is that when a small child tears a plant from the ground, a parent's first reaction should be to say, "No, don't touch that." The child's first reaction is likely to be, "But why?" This parenting class taught me to say, "No, don't touch that because if everyone grabbed flowers, there would be no flowers in the world." It's just looking at it from a different perspective and honoring the question they asked.

Somewhere along the way, we stop asking those childlike "why" questions. When we allow someone to mentor us, we have to reawaken our natural curiosity about life. Our independent, do-it-yourself culture may be losing the art of mentoring because we are too scared to ask for help and advice. We also experience fewer opportunities to mentor others because no one is asking us any questions either! We are all guilty of contributing to an epidemic of ignorance and stagnation.

Look Who You're Asking

Why do we ask people in the same boat as us for advice? Many successful people are more than willing to share their ideas with others. Once their cup is full, they have more to share and they want to share it. It's lonely at the top!

Find the person who seems to have, do, and be more of whatever it is that you want in life and start asking questions. With any of my goals, I have always looked for a mentor, whether the goal is financial, social, spiritual, or physical. If I want to lose weight, I would ask someone who has succeeded in a healthy diet and weight-loss program. If I wanted to pursue a new business venture, I would ask a successful businessperson. It is a lot easier to follow a path that somebody else has already traveled.

We often don't tap into a source of success that is right in front of us - our family. They tend to be valuable advisors, as they understand our background and can tailor their advice to fit us better. If we think we only inherit our physical genetics, we are sadly mistaken. One of the things I wish we did more of as a society is to learn from each other, generation to generation. We need to take the time to interview our mothers and fathers and grandparents to determine the important lessons they have learned about life, relationships, business, and success. One would think that we should improve from one generation to the next, but we tend to repeat ineffective patterns because we don't ask and, as a result, we don't learn.

Ask Mentors Specific Questions

I have never ceased to have mentors, and I still ask as many questions as I need to reach my goals. Recently, I called a man at the largest financial planning firm in Canada. He is sixty-seven years old and an expert in acquisitions in an area similar to the one I want to specialize in. I did not know him, but I told him what I was attempting to do and said,

"I would like to learn from someone who has been there." I asked my two favorite questions: "Do you think that anyone can learn from their mistakes, but a wise person learns from other people's mistakes? And do you think that when the student is ready, the teacher will appear?" He laughed, but the next thing I knew he was on a plane to Texas to meet with me.

He graciously shared many of the things he had discovered along the way, including valuable lessons he had learned from his mistakes. He helped to clarify the dos and don'ts. If I had pursued the acquisition phase of business on my own, I would have probably made some costly mistakes trying to figure out what he already knew to avoid. His insights equipped me with the confidence I needed to proceed with my own endeavors. Once he had agreed to meet with me, I took the time to write down my goals and detail exactly what I wanted this success to look like. If you are able to let a potential mentor know exactly what you are trying to accomplish, they will often be glad to help you attain your goals.

I asked him everything: *What makes you tick? What lessons did you learn along the way?* When you pick someone up at the airport, the first question you usually ask is, "How was your trip?" Similarly, when you see someone who has achieved something you want to, ask them, "How did you do it?" If you want to be the best at something, find someone who is already excelling in it and ask them how they did it.

Have Several Mentors to Gain Different Perspectives

Having mentors in several areas of our lives allows us to

grow faster than if we were to do it on our own. Different aspects of life require different mentors, but the overriding principle is the same: if we are prepared to learn, our mentors can give us wings. Like good books, each of them contains a gem waiting to be uncovered. They also overlap; the person we think of as a business mentor may very well turn out to offer us some of the wisest life lessons to be had. Good mentors are wise shortcuts; reinventing the wheel has no merit, but standing on the shoulders of another can make giants of both participants.

It works the same way with books; one good book may introduce you to two or three others that all contribute different perspectives on the same topic.

Questions We Rarely Ask

Have you heard the proverb, "To be understood, one must first seek to understand?" For me, to be a lifelong learner and keep asking questions, I have to ensure that I listen attentively. Thanks to my brother John, I have learned to listen to people, keeping my mouth shut and my ears and eyes open. People are drawn to someone who values what they have to say. Being a good communicator often means being absolutely quiet. Stillness speaks.

On the other hand, people shut down when they come across as know-it-alls or fix-its; they have nothing to add and so they withdraw. Assuming we know everything about someone else or their situation without asking any questions conveys the message that "I don't care enough to let you tell me." I often see couples and families in my office who have never discussed their feelings about important issues, but the frustration and hurt in their responses is evident.

"Why Is That Important to You?"

I once knew a man whose sole motivation for his financial strategies was to create more security for himself and his family. It was very important to him, as he had not had any sense of financial security growing up. His wife, however, had come from a different experience; she had grown up in a wealthy family where financial security was never a concern - it was a given. Her philosophy was, "Everything will be alright no matter how much you spend."

This gap in their understanding proved to be a major obstacle in their relationship. She would scold her husband because he was always questioning every financial move they made. If she bought something expensive, it would drive her crazy that he would worry about whether they could really afford it (which they could). Likewise, he could not understand why an issue that was so important to him seemed irrelevant to her. They talked about money constantly, but they never asked each other what that one little word meant to either of them.

When this couple went through the process of discovering their unique personal values and what was most important to them about money, they realized their core issue was linked to how they had been raised. She finally understood for the first time why he had been asking all the questions that had caused conflict in the marriage. Meanwhile, he realized how his wife's family had influenced her thinking about money.

Once they began to ask each other questions about what

was important to each of them, they were both more open to the other's perspective now that they understood the "why" behind their actions. This changed their marriage; she no longer felt threatened by the questions, and he no longer resented her spending money. They learned that loving each other meant that he needed to understand what was important to her, just as she needed to understand his feelings about the need for security.

Too often, we hold ourselves back when we don't ask for what we want from others, and we don't try to understand their perspective. We create a whole library of false beliefs, resentments, and unnecessary concerns from bad information (or the lack of it).

"Do You Understand What I Need From You?"

Whenever there is a breakdown in communication at home or at work, we must start asking questions. It is easy to misconstrue the facts when one does not ask questions; this is usually the case when something does not get done or something goes wrong.

When I'm part of a communication breakdown, the first thing I do is ask myself if I have clearly communicated my expectations. When I present information to a group or individual, I always ask for feedback to ensure that they understand what I want. I may not have communicated my thoughts effectively, or the listeners may have interpreted the information differently. To ensure that communication is clear, I cannot assume anything. Asking someone, "Do you understand?" is not as effective as asking them to explain what they have heard in their own words.

"Why Do You Ask?"

When I was a young man starting out in business, whenever someone asked me my opinion, I would blurt it out without thinking. For instance, if someone asked me my opinion about a certain football coach, I would tell them exactly what I thought. More often than not, I ended up putting my foot in my mouth because I had just insulted their favorite team! One day, a good friend of mine told me, "Whenever someone asks you for your personal opinion, you should say 'Why do you ask?' so that you won't get your foot stuck in your mouth!"

That one piece of advice has helped me immensely, as that small sentence draws a wealth of information and puts the question back in the hands of the original questioner. More information and facts equip one to make wiser decisions. If I say, "Why do you ask?" That person might tell me they are a raving fan of that team and I will know what not to say! By saying, "Why do you ask?" I can understand the motives behind their question.

"Why Not?"

As I look at everything I have or do not yet have in my life in terms of success, I often ask myself one important question: Why not? Why am I not doing what I dreamed I would be doing by now?

Among the many inspiring quotes I have been heard over the years, I remember seeing a documentary about Robert F. Kennedy giving a speech at a campaign rally in Indianapolis, Indiana, which he began by paraphrasing the Irish playwright George Bernard Shaw:

"There are those that look at things the way they are, and ask,' Why?' I dream of things that never were, and ask 'Why not?' The future does not belong to those who are content with today, apathetic toward common problems and their fellow man alike, timid and fearful in the face of bold projects and new ideas. Rather, it will belong to those who can blend passion, reason and courage in a personal commitment to the great enterprises and ideals of American society."
- Robert F. Kennedy

Partnering with People and Building the Impossible

"Coming together is a beginning; keeping together is progress; working together is success."
- Henry Ford

Baseball is one of my passions, and I was heartbroken when I found out that my city had planned to demolish an historic ballpark and turn it into a parking lot. The stadium, boasting a seating capacity of 4,000, was unusual for Tyler in the 1940s. Back then, Tyler was just a little East Texas town outside of Big D, Dallas. Still, it had been the home of several professional, semi-professional, and collegiate baseball teams dating all the way back to 1941.

I began to follow the efforts to save this historic stadium with interest. Some city leaders petitioned the Tyler City Council for $25,000 to make much-needed renovations, but were summarily turned down.

I happened to be at that meeting, and afterwards, I asked

the petitioner what all needed to be done to the park to bring it back to life. He rattled off a list that included major projects like painting the walls and repairing the dugout and stadium seats. That night, I couldn't stop thinking about how much our community would lose by destroying such an important part of East Texas history. I decided I would at least push it a little further to see if there was any hope of restoring it to its former glory.

By the next morning, I couldn't take it any longer. I went to Hightower Lumber Company alone and met with a man who agreed to accompany me to the ballpark to see the project for himself.

When we arrived, we parked on an old, potholed blacktop that served as a parking lot, and we walked onto the field. A couple of stray cats darted out from the dugouts, and the wind whipped up the dirt and weeds growing freely on the pitcher's mound. It was hard to even imagine a day when these broken metal seats had held thousands of cheering fans rooting for the home team.

We made quite a pair that day-he in his coveralls and me in my business suit. We turned our attention first to the dugouts that were now warped and worn. It looked bad-almost hopeless. Nevertheless, I tried to stay positive and asked, "So, what kind of lumber do we need to build out these dugouts?"

To make matters worse, he and I both knew that there was no budget for any of this because the plans to demolish it had been in the newspaper for quite some time. So, in exchange for his lumber and labor, I made him an offer that I was sure he couldn't refuse. I proudly told him I would give the lumber company a 19x14 ad on the outfield wall once we were up and running again.

He smiled politely and kicked up some dirt with the toe of his boot. Squinting in the morning sun, he put his hands in his pockets and said slowly, "Son, I don't really want an ad on the wall."

I was devastated. Looking back, he must have thought I was completely out of my mind to even dream of restoring this old park. What kind of lumber would it take? Not free lumber, after all. He knew I didn't have any money for this, so that didn't really leave me much to barter with.

"Sure, I understand," I began. "I apologize for wasting your time."

"I don't really want an ad on the wall," he repeated. "But I want to help you if I can. I've always had a dream for what this field could be."

The next day, several trucks from his company rumbled onto the blacktop and dropped off load after load of prime lumber in front of the dugouts. The dream was beginning to take shape.

I had a fraternity brother at the time who was in the construction business, and it just so happened that he knew how to set and build the dugouts. Within a matter of days, we had permission from the city to begin construction. A whole crew of volunteers came with their sleeves rolled up and their hard hats on. Our first task was to sand the old paint off the outfield fence in order to prepare it for a fresh coat. As I sanded off those huge flakes of dried paint and dirt, I smiled imagining all the home runs that had soared over that fence in the past sixty years. It looked like the

home runs would keep on flying.

Before the project was over, I had convinced several other local companies and individuals to purchase a few of the 9x14 signs on the fence to help us out. Finally, when the facelift was completed with new stadium seats, new dugouts, and a renewed field, we had spent less than $900. In other words, when we volunteered and teamed up with other partners, we had accomplished the same project that had been estimated to cost $25,000! There is no way to underestimate the value of good partnerships.

I learned a valuable lesson through this experience: *it is better to work together than to work alone.* People are willing to participate in your dreams if you let them. There is something inside each of us that longs to attempt the impossible and make a difference.

If you show people a dream and explain the value of their contribution and *how* they can make a difference, they will usually sign up quickly. They just need to look beyond the *cost* of their commitment to the *impact* they can make.

When a noble endeavor is involved, most partners won't ask for anything in return. Our world is full of people just waiting to be asked to be a part of something incredible.

Principles for Partnering with Others

Teamwork is one of the most powerful forces in our world, impacting every area of our lives. When I coached little league football, the parents would often pull me aside after practice to thank me, saying things like, "This football team is more than just a sport for my son. It has given him direction and structure in his life for the first time, and now he has dreams."

My children were all from an underprivileged neighborhood, and what they had learnt on the field had a positive effect on their everyday lives. I will never forget how proud (and shocked) the mothers were when they told me their sons were now cleaning their rooms and helping around the house with chores. They were doing better in school and making more positive choices.

I often think that God must have wanted us to work as teams because He put us in families right away. No baby is born alone; there are no Lone Rangers in the hospital nursery. Even he had Tonto! From the moment we're born, we depend on others to help us learn to live life to its fullest. Why do we think we should make it alone when we're older? There are several principles I've learned about partnering with other people to achieve more in life.

Learning to Care for Each Other

Football is fun and good for physical development, but

it is also where my players learned the value of teamwork. They weren't just a bunch of individuals out on the field when we worked and played together - they were part of a team. Each player needed the other to succeed. When one person scored, the whole team benefited. We shared all the ups and downs and found out that each team member had the potential to positively affect another.

There were times when some of my players felt like quitting. They thought the game was too hard, or they were frustrated by their lack of progress. It made me proud when I saw the other kids encouraging them in their own childlike ways to keep going. We all have to learn to trust each other during difficult times in our lives. It works the same way on a little league football team as it does in a family of four or a Fortune 500 organization.

I have also discovered the value of this principle as a husband. I have learned how important it is for me to trust my wife when she makes a decision related to our child. It is one way I can show her that we are on the same team. We once took a parenting class called "Growing Kids God's Way", where we learned that the unity of a mother and father affects a child. Communicating that unity to our daughter makes her feel safe, and there are no sides for her to choose.

A child becomes an extension of the bond between their parents. Supporting and caring for one another means we are winning together as a family.

Finding Out What's Important To Others

One of my coworkers was struggling with unmanageable debt. She had tried, unsuccessfully, to sell her house and the situation was suffocating her. We sat down to consider her options and, together, began to map the way out of debt and into her dreams. By the time we finished, she was breathing a lot easier and there was even a hint of a smile.

This co-worker implemented her plan with enthusiasm, and I saw something incredible happen over the next two months. Making positive decisions in her financial life had an impact on her emotionally, and this carried over to an improved attitude towards her work. Instead of being depressed, she began to show tremendous pride in her work. I learned I could depend on her completely, and she became an extremely loyal employee.

Helping people gain clarity about their goals is key to partnering. When you help others grow, your own growth is inevitable. Mapping out the things that are important to them and showing them ways to implement the steps necessary to reach their fullest potential is one of the most fulfilling parts of my life.

I realized a long time ago that none of my employees are forced to work for me; they can work anywhere they choose. In reality, they are working for themselves, through my business, to attain their own goals, dreams, and desires. If I can help them develop a game plan to achieve their goals, chances are they will return the favor by helping me to achieve mine.

I treat my customers, vendors, and employees the same way, partnering with each of them for the best results for all of us.

Of course, you'll always find people who have little or no self-motivation. For them, making a paycheck to pay their bills is the big picture. These are some of my favorite people. I love to watch the look on their faces the first time they discover there is a big goal out there with their name on it. My reward is showing them how to move from the only picture they know to a much larger one.

Communicating the Game Plan

Another principle for partnering with others requires that the game plan be clear to everyone on the team; every successful team understands the overall game plan. Some businesses call it a mission statement, but I don't just limit it to the workplace; even our family has its own mission statement, which describes our values and defines where we're going.

Many poorly-run organizations are filled with people who are clueless about the team's game plan; they have no clue about the specific role they should play. It's like the story I heard about two men who were struggling to get a bulky piece of furniture through a narrow door; they were grunting and groaning to make it fit. One man said, "We almost have it in," and at that point, the guy on the other end said, "In? I thought we were trying to get it out." A leader's challenge is to communicate the overall game plan clearly in any endeavor.

Assigning Roles of the Team

Getting people into the right positions in an organization is crucial. This means breaking down the plan for success into its different components and determining which role best fits each individual. On my little league team, there were many different positions for the kids to play. At the start of each season, everyone wanted to be the quarterback, but a team cannot function with eleven quarterbacks on the field. My task was to explain the importance of each position. Once that was accomplished, everything just fell into place.

You can always tell when your team understands their role in the big game plan. Once the roles and expectations are clear and everyone respects each other, it creates a high-performance team in a positive and creative environment. When this happens, your team is unstoppable and anything becomes possible!

Recognizing Contributions to the Team

Everyone enjoys recognition for a job well done. As a coach, one of my most important tasks was to recognize my players' strengths and weaknesses, and then capitalize on their strengths. A successful team is a group of successful individuals, each working in their area of expertise.

We all have the same goal: to participate in and win the game. Recognizing individual accomplishments encourages everyone to constantly strive for their personal best. Recognizing contributions to the success of the overall game encourages people to work harder together.

Realizing It's Easier To Work Together Than Apart

Coming from a close-knit family who overcame difficult odds and now work together in the same business, we have all realized that *it is easier to work together than apart.*

Many brothers and sisters have just the opposite experience; they do not get along well or even talk to each other. However, our experiences have brought us closer together. We approach every opportunity with positive expectations, and we go from there together.

Those who try to work alone seldom reach their full potential. Masterminding is simply creating a third mind when two people come up with several good ideas that lead to even greater ones. There is always someone else in your office, in your neighborhood, in your class, etc. who wants to achieve the same goals as you.

I remember, as a kid, running from house to house looking for someone to come out and play. Sometimes we built forts, and sometimes we got splinters in our fingers while trying to put together a rickety old tree house. Whatever we did, we were just out there playing together. That's how I feel about work too.

If you approach work that way, the pressure is off and misery is avoided. When we view our job as a game, we strive to play it well with everyone around us. True success is achieved when our job is a joy rather than a chore.

Just Ask

Partnering with other people has opened more doors of opportunity than I could have ever experienced if I had done things on my own.

I often ask myself, "What am I currently doing in my life and/or business that is so outrageous that I can only achieve it if I partner with others? How might I be limiting my dreams if I don't share my vision?"

I wonder what would have happened if I had never asked

the lumber company to come and see the baseball stadium through our eyes. We both saw the vision that day. I might have missed out on a great opportunity to collaborate simply because I did not ask.

2 Hour House

"None of us is as smart as all of us."
- Ken Blanchard

A great example of partnering with people and building the impossible is the 2-Hour House.
A few years ago, my friend and client Brian Conaway was set to become the chairman of the Tyler Texas Area Builders Association, and was looking for a way to increase the Association's membership for the following year. But, sometimes a simple idea can make a real difference. The Association's membership did grow that year, but in the meantime, his idea to increase membership resulted in industry competitors banding together as volunteers to do something very special for the community. He ended up breaking a world record, creating a remarkable showcase for his industry, and changing the way everyone involved viewed their lives.

He had seen a news story about a house in California being built in three hours, forty-four minutes, and fifty-nine seconds, and the more he looked at that project, the more he realized he could build a house in less time. In fact, he figured with the right number of volunteers, he could build a 2,300-square-foot house that would exceed code in less than three hours.

You see, Brian realized that with enough pre-planning and attention to detail, by identifying local tradespeople and suppliers with vision and a passion for excellence, and by motivating hundreds of volunteers to be part of this near-impossible project, a whole lot of lives could be changed for the better.

Remarkably, he wanted to build a 2,300-square-foot house from start to finish in the time it takes to watch Monday Night Football. Imagine all the lumber, fixtures, and wiring, all the building materials that were used to build the house you live in today. Every sheet of wallboard and drop of paint was sitting in an empty lot waiting for the construction crew to arrive. And he expected to return to that empty lot, after playing eighteen holes of golf, to his brand new house complete with landscaping.

Having a vision of what we want to accomplish in life is the easy part of our journey. Brian's idea of building a house to increase his association's membership and benefit a local charity was great. But we all have great ideas, or at least ideas that we think are great. The real obstacle in wanting to build a house in less than three hours was realizing that it couldn't be done unless he could successfully inspire nearly 600 tradesmen, suppliers, and volunteers to challenge themselves to liberate their minds from thinking that dreams cannot come true, to knowing that we are all destined for remarkable and unprecedented growth.

Now, one of the reasons I was motivated to succeed in life was that I'm not very handy around the house and I looked forward to the day when I wouldn't have to fix the leaky water heater. Considering that it takes me about 20 minutes to figure out how to change a light bulb, the thought of building a 2300 square-foot house in the time it would take me to change nine light bulbs blew my mind. It wasn't easy convincing a group of skilled construction tradesmen that it could be done either.

Even the most experienced worker will tell you they need a day or two to set the forms and dig the footings for the foundation before the concrete is poured and finished, which takes a full day to do it right. Then you have to pop the lines before setting the walls, which is going to take a day. And at least another day on top of that to frame the walls.

Figure a half-day to rough-in the plumbing and a full day to rough-in the electrical. Then, another day to put in the wall plumbing, as up until now we only did a rough-in.

Now the walls and roof need to be insulated so everything can be sheet-rocked – before spending the next four days taping and texturing the walls. And all that needs to be done before another crew arrives on-site to paint. Figure at least two days for the paint.

What about kitchen cabinets? The bathroom fixtures? The heating and cooling system? The interior doors and baseboards? The countertops? The floors? Did we even talk about the ceilings?

Assuming the weather cooperated, and the different

work crews showed up on time, and all the raw materials were always ready and waiting on site, we're already weeks into our project -- and we haven't even talked about all those little things that go into the interior of a house.

What about the exterior of the house? We need at least a day for the final grade, and another to lay the grass. And yet another half-day to install the garage door.

Did we remember to shingle the roof? If we didn't, figure on another day for that.

And my friend Brian wants to do all this in less than three hours.

The Herman Report suggests that 80% of all Americans work at 40% of their capacity because they don't have a strong belief in their true potential. This suggests that creating a challenging and stimulating work environment can make immediate and extraordinary changes in the human spirit and, more remarkably, have a profound influence on our success potential.

This is why the 2 Hour House project was so intriguing. Brian had to imagine the completed house and then back into the project, detailing each element and giving the crew chiefs the maximum amount of time they would have to accomplish their goal.

He didn't tell the crew chiefs how to do what they needed to do, but rather how much time they could take and where their area of expertise fit into the master plan. He was the outsider, the one not directly involved with their process, who took them out of their comfort zone and inspired their true potential.

Before constructing the house, every part of it had to be

deconstructed. Coordinating and communicating with 600 volunteers who had less than three hours to work together and complete a 2300 square foot house was daunting. Inspiring workers to change the way they had always done their jobs and move past their comfort zone to create new processes and procedures was difficult, but doable.

He relied on each individual's passion for what they did best. A few years ago, I read a Harvard Business School study about individual strengths and weaknesses and how these variables affect productivity. So, we went to every employee in the firm and asked them to list all the things they loved to do at work and what was a burden. After reviewing the results, we found that tasks that were one employee's weakness - something they might do on a daily or weekly basis that they weren't thrilled about doing - was another employee's strength, sometimes even their passion. And by making minor changes to a number of job descriptions, the result was an almost immediate and sustainable 15% increase in productivity company-wide.

In our business and sometimes personal lives, we have a tendency to focus on the negative and try to improve on our weaknesses, instead of running with our strengths. And I realized that by making minor changes to those job descriptions, we were turning one employee's "work" into another employee's "play". And when you have a culture of play in the workplace, it is truly amazing how productive and creative people can be on their way to becoming the best version of themselves.

How many times in our life do we focus on a weakness? In the perfect world of our minds, we want our kids to succeed in life, so some of us expect them to come home with straight A's. When their report card has three A's, one B, and a C, we tend to focus on the C, when we should be celebrating the three A's and the B.

Just like in the Harvard study, is that C a simple example of strengths and weaknesses? Maybe they don't like the teacher, or something or someone is disruptive in class, or maybe they just don't like the subject.

I always make it a point to ask my daughter to tell me two things that she is really proud of today. If you start to do the same, you'll notice that at first the person needs to stop and really search for the answer. Most people can tell you everything that went wrong during the day, but most of us have difficulty remembering what went right and what we are proud of. It takes practice to train ourselves to focus on the positive, but I promise you it will change the way you look at yourself, your accomplishments, and the way you look at the future.

Which is why I am such a fan of the 2 Hour House project. It changed the way every one of those 600 volunteers looked at themselves and their accomplishments, and I think it changed how they look at their future in a profound way. They were the direct beneficiaries of the power of delegation.

You see, Brian recognized what we all need to understand: that sometimes, other people can do it better and faster than we can. This, in turn, allows us to focus on the things in life that are most important to us. It also reminds us that we can all turn an impossible into a possible with innovation, planning, and creative thinking.

Just look at what they achieved: building a 2,300-square-

foot house that exceeded code in 2 hours and 52 minutes. A brand-new three-bedroom ranch standing where an empty lot was just the day before.

Success sometimes requires us to refuse to accept our perceived business and personal limitations. Just like with the house, by challenging ourselves daily to liberate our "entrapped mind" - which only serves to tell us that dreams cannot come true - we are all destined for remarkable and unprecedented growth.

Each House is Different

The 2 Hour House helped me realize why success means different things to each of us. Our homes represent what is most important to us. Younger families may want a two-story home for the extra room, while empty nesters are downsizing as quickly as possible. There may be twenty homes on a city block, but each one has a different layout and different colored walls, carpets, counters, and floors. All you have to do is look around the neighborhood to realize that we are all different. And yet, we all want peace of mind and success in life, and to know that we are making an impact. Peace of mind means different things to different people.

What does an ideal business look like to each one of my employees? Probably not the way I envisage it. It is important to me to ask others what success means to them and understand it from their vantage point. What does success look like from the sales perspective? What represents success in the tech department? Each area will have a different definition. Whenever I partner with people, I try to remember that we are all unique, and we all want different things.

Opening the Doors of Opportunity

Partnering with other people has opened more doors of opportunity than I could have ever experienced if I had done things on my own.

During the two years of preparation for the 2 Hour House, Brian shared the vision with hundreds of volunteers who each contributed a part. Imagine hundreds of people looking at the same house from different perspectives. An electrician would have seen something entirely different from what the carpet layer or cabinet installer saw. An engineer would have had a different vantage point than an architect and vice versa.

Sharing his vision resulted in something much greater than he could have accomplished on his own. Reams of paper captured every trade expert's perspective on how to get their part of the project done in the least amount of time possible. When Brian combined all of these perspectives into one master plan, the result was infinitely better than a single viewpoint.

I often ask myself, "What am I currently doing in my life and/or business that is so outrageous that I can only achieve it if I partner with others? How might I be limiting my dreams if I don't share my vision?"

Our Holistic Practice

"The key to financial success is to view money as a tool to help you achieve your goals, not as an end in itself."
- Suze Orman

More and more, our future financial success will be dependent on how quickly we can adapt to the marketplace and the specific demands of our life. Every decision you make with money affects something else.

Managing one's finances can be a complex and challenging task. There are numerous financial decisions that individuals need to make throughout their lives, from saving for retirement to paying for education or buying a house.

I mentioned this because most consumers have accumulated a collection of investments over the years and, as a result, have a large number of professionals advising them. The problem is that none of these professionals are communicating with each other about the client's overall plan. Nothing is connected or clearly organized, meaning our

prospects are usually paying more than they need to, as they are paying the overhead for eight people instead of one.

Many people struggle with the decisions they need to make regarding money. That is why we have created a process to simplify their finances and give them a plan so that they can feel organized. We want people to live life with purpose, to feel safe, secure, and in control. As a holistic financial planning firm, we can provide invaluable assistance in navigating these decisions, creating a personalized financial plan that aligns with individual goals and objectives, and taking into account various financial considerations and risks.

The mission of the Feliciano Financial Group is to inspire and motivate people to be proactive and to live their lives with purpose. To that end, we have spent the last 20 years working towards developing a holistic wealth management firm that supports our clients in thinking through what they really want to achieve in life and looking at the big picture.

When referring to our Holistic approach, we mean

having Tax Planning, Investment, Insurance Planning, Retirement Planning, Estate Planning, Cash Flow, Budgeting, and Business Planning all under one roof. However, according to the most recent available data, only about 6.6% of all financial advisors in the country offer it.

Holistic financial planning is not just about money; it's about the decisions a client makes with money and the impact those decisions have on what they want out of life. When we plan, we want to find the "why" before we discuss the "what".

In addition, being an independent firm gives us the freedom to help people. We are not confined to any one product or financial strategy, as every plan is unique. We are independent people, with a can-do attitude. We take responsibility for finding the best solution for the client, demonstrating discipline, and working hard because we love what we do and the people we serve.

Good relationships are built on trust and staying true to oneself. We aim to be open, transparent, honest, and direct in all our actions. For the past 35 years, the mission of the Feliciano Financial Group has been to inspire and motivate people to take action and live their lives with purpose.

Planning and Achieving Your Greatest Goals

"If you don't know where you are going,
you'll end up someplace else."
- Yogi Berra

They came into my office holding a check from an oil and gas lease. This couple, older clients of our firm, had been saving for years but had no formal financial plan. They had no idea if they were "safe" or not. When they came to us, I sat with them and really listened. Together, we identified their dreams and goals. Within a short time, we had customized a master plan that structured their financial affairs. Just how well-organized their finances were now would only become apparent to them later on - in fact, the day they walked into my office holding that check.

I could tell from the look on their faces that this was just a routine deposit into another investment to keep them safe. They had done well financially, but they had forgotten the purpose of that plan: reaching their goals and fulfilling their dreams.

Ironically, the couple in this story were exactly where they wanted to be financially, as they had been diligently following the financial plan we had created together. However, up to this point, they had never taken the time to celebrate, create memories, and enjoy life - the very things that financial stability allows us to do.

Sitting across from them at the table that day, I looked up and asked, "Why don't you take this money and go on a lifetime trip?" They looked at each other wide-eyed and then turned to look back at me.

"Could we?" The man asked doubtfully, scratching his chin. His wife looked from him to me and back to him in disbelief. I showed them again where they were financially; everything had been accomplished according to plan. Now it was time for them to begin enjoying the fruits of their diligent plan. I'm happy to say that two months later they were taking pictures in front of the Sydney Opera House in Australia.

Enjoying the Adventure

The greatest enjoyment in my career is helping people plan for and experience a great life. When I ask people what having a great life means to them, I hear a number of different answers. Some want to be wealthy and have the freedom to invest in the future of others; some want to have an intimate family life; some want to travel; others want security for them and their families. It does not matter what religion, ethnicity, background, or nationality defines us; we all have a common desire to experience inner peace and know without a doubt that we have had some kind of impact on the world. I have one caveat along the way: sometimes life brings us unplanned surprises, and in their own way, they are just as important as planning a great life. Sometimes, they are the rewards that keep us focused.

In my business, a lot of what we do begins with helping others rediscover for themselves what is most important to them. They know it; they just have forgotten it along the way. For me, it is just as important to design the steps as it is to design the goal.

Everyone has ideas and values that are sacred - things that never fail to make them smile, bring a sigh of relief, or dare to dream. These are the steps that keep us on track with the bigger picture. Sometimes we think we have to wait until something falls into place for those to happen, but not always.

Recently, a father and son sat down in my office to talk about the inheritance the teenager had received. He wanted to save for the future. I asked the son, "What is important to you about money?"

"Feeling secure," he answered cautiously and then his eyes lit up. "I have always wanted to visit the Smithsonian," he blurted out and then subsided again.

His father leaned forward and looked at his son. "What did you say?" he asked. "The Smithsonian?"

"I've always wanted to go to the Smithsonian," the son replied. A different kid was sitting in front of me now, their eyes bright with excitement.

Dumbfounded, the father looked at his teenage son.

"Son," he said, "I never knew you wanted to do that." They invested the money wisely, but there was a light in the father's eyes that had not been there before.

Three weeks later, they returned from a father-and-son trip to the Northeast that they would never forget. Their story reminds me that we all need to talk to each other about what we most want to do and experience in life. These are the things we should share with one another. All too often, we bury the things that are most important. The more you dream and share what you plan to do with the precious gift of life, the further you are likely to go.

Great Lives Take Planning

It's astonishing how hard it is sometimes to write down the goals that are important to you. Even putting something like a simple timeline on our goals can be a new exercise for some people. Putting it on paper makes it real, creates confidence, eliminates negativity and convinces your subconscious mind that you can accomplish whatever you set out to do.

Unfortunately, we don't learn this early on in life. In school, we rarely teach children how to manage their time, money, and other resources to help them achieve their dreams.

Most people live life saying, "If I had this, I could be that." That is not true. I have found that when you learn to "be" the person you want to be, or "be" the company you want to be and "do" the things you need to do in order to make that happen, then you will "have" what you want to have. In that order.

We are taught not to dream too big or reach too high, so as not to set ourselves up for disappointment. We should not bite off more than we can chew. However, too often, "Don't" becomes "What's the use?", and we stop having any sort of plan for our lives, simply letting life happen. We get jobs and soon forget about having a passion for careers or dreams, not thinking we should love our work, and losing sight of what we are really working for.

Many people stop dreaming at the point of money; however, it does not take money to fuel one's dreams. Time is the primary currency that powers our dreams, and the root cause of not achieving them is failing to use one's time wisely. Time is the primary currency for success; focus is second; money is last. The wise and diligent application of all three will lead to success.

In other words, a great life doesn't just happen on its own; you have to plan for it. Don't miss out on the unimaginably large rewards of disciplined planning as you push forward into the realm of all that your life could be. Spend a moment reflecting on and planning your dreams before you spend a dollar; the wise investment of your time will yield a more profitable return.

The Truth About Goals

Before you start writing down some of your goals, you need to know what constitutes a good one.

Goals are not the same as desires. Goals represent those things over which you have personal control; desires are simply what you would like the outcome to be. Some people confuse the two. You might say one of your goals in life is to raise great kids. However, something that requires someone else to conform to your wishes is not a good goal; rather, that would be more of a desire. Desires often require someone else to help fulfill them. What if your kids make decisions you don't agree with? What if they choose a path other than the one you had in mind for them?

Be sure that the goals you have for your life do not involve the desire to change someone else's. We do not have permission to change other people. At most, we have the power to initiate real change when someone sees us accomplish our own goals and feels inspired to want more out of life too. Whatever you choose to be, do, or have - regardless of others' behavior - is a true goal.

A Goal Must Tap Into Your Passions

One of the most important questions I ask people about their life goals is: "How will you feel once you have accomplished them?" If that person is not enthusiastic about accomplishing their goals, it is either too small or simply unexciting.

If you cannot connect with the emotions you would experience once you achieve your life goals, you will not have the motivation to accomplish them. Most of us run out of energy far before we reach our destination. It is not that our dreams are too ambitious - it is that they are too insignificant! Even worse, we fail to refuel regularly to keep the journey going.

I often ask people to tell me why achieving their goals is important to them so they can tap into their passion. I believe the following formula is true: Discovering Why - Creates More Passion - Fulfills Goals. For example, we all know it is important to save money and have enough to meet our needs. However, we all have different opinions on why that is important to us. Knowing why creates more passion for fulfilling our goals.

Knowing why we want to save money will reveal what drives us. Some people are driven by past experience; I have heard people say, "I was poor when I was growing up and I never want to go back there." Consider why you have certain goals in life, and you will start to comprehend what you are passionate about and what motivates you. You will also start to understand that for each of us, "money" is a stand-in for a range of freedoms.

A Goal is Personal and Sacrosanct

For me, it is important that the goals I have are things I want to achieve, not what others expect of me. Constantly worrying about what everyone expects would impede my ability to set big goals. I would have too many factors to consider and would likely become overwhelmed. Life goals are inviolable. Within the dreamer lies the place where happiness and the capability to achieve lies.

If you go into a career that you didn't choose and didn't want, it is no wonder you don't feel passionate about it. You have to pursue what you love doing in order to be able to set personal goals that make you eager to get out of bed every day, excited to take those goals another step further. I only pursue things I have a passion for, in areas that highlight my strengths.

A Goal Requires Action

Many of us outline our goals but don't take any action to make them happen - it's like having the keys to a beautiful car that you never drive anywhere. Some people are afraid to take action because they fear failure, believing that a car in the garage is safer than a car in motion. However, there will always be challenges and unforeseen obstacles, and it is impossible to anticipate where the bottlenecks are until we start taking action. An old saying goes, "Do what you fear most and you control fear". Furthermore, most of what you fear happening only exists in your mind.

So, what if you decide to do nothing? Inactivity is not as neutral as it sounds - it is a conscious decision to not move forward in our lives. When we take no action, we are going against the flow of life that naturally wants to move us forward and to be, do, and have more than we presently experience. It actually takes more energy to do nothing; it's like treading water - you're not going anywhere, but it still takes a lot of time and energy to keep afloat.

I want to be more like the people I see at an airport. When I travel, I see people dressed for the beach and businessmen in power suits all boarding the same plane. One person is shoving a beach bag into the overhead compartment next to a businesswoman balancing her computer and a month's worth of paperwork in her lap.

We may look different, but everybody in an airport has one thing in common: they are all going somewhere. From the business people in power suits to the vacationers heading to Bermuda, every person in the terminal is headed somewhere in their lives. They are either going somewhere intentionally or allowing life to take them to the next thing. No one is standing still. We are all people in motion, either intentionally or reactively.

Mapping: Living Your Life on Purpose

In some ways, financial planning is similar to a charter travel agency; we help people plan or map the best route to their desired destinations in their personal lives. People who have a passion for possibilities develop a clear vision for their lives and follow a map to get there.

Maps show us where we've been, where we are, and most importantly, where to go next. If you were driving from Texas to Indiana, you could look at a climate map, a topographical map, and a resource map, but none of those maps would get you there. On a road trip, you would use a highway map or road atlas to get to your destination.

"The map matters! How we reach our destination depends on the clarity of the map we create. If you don't know where you are going, any map will take you there. Creating the right map or plan for your goals will be strategically important for your success."

People who believe in the power of possibilities are modern-day cartographers; they are map-makers who chart their way to new, unexplored worlds and dimensions waiting patiently to be discovered in their lives.

A large part of our personal map relates to how we grew up. My map is different from yours; you are the sole author, discoverer, and compiler of that map, and only you know how it should look.

The Right Map Makes Your Priorities Clear

I've helped people create road maps for tangible goals like personal wealth, but the greater thrill is the byproduct of good maps that enhance the less tangible areas of our lives.

Take marriage relationships as an example. One day, a husband and wife sat in my office. He was a doctor and they enjoyed a comfortable lifestyle. However, the husband was extremely frustrated by his wife's spending habits and they were not communicating effectively about this issue.

We spent a lot of time talking about their dreams and what was important to them. They described wanting to plan for college for their children and maintaining a certain lifestyle in retirement. The wife shared how important it was to give to others and support good causes because of the peace of mind she gained from doing so. She also always wanted to be in a position to help her family when needed.

However, a major problem arose when we laid out the plan for their future. The wife's spending rate threatened those future goals, and credit card debt was mounting. When she was sitting in my office that day, she understood for the first time that her current actions would soon sabotage her future goals.

As the realization sank in, she sat up straight, looked each of us in the eye and asked for a pair of scissors. She then reached into her purse, took eight credit cards out of her wallet and cut them to pieces on my conference room table.

When we are committed to putting our plans on paper and living with purpose, everything in life fits together. We can finally see the delicate balance of how every value we hold dear and every decision we make affects everything else.

Clear Vision Brings Easier Decisions

It is amazing what can happen when you have a clear vision and follow the plan. Roy Disney, Walt Disney's brother and co-founder of Disneyland, once said, "When your vision is clear, your decisions are easy." Decisions become easier in all aspects of life.

Returning to the marathon, vision and decision-making are especially important for runners. You won't find serious marathon competitors contemplating what else they could be doing with their time. They are solely focused on running.

They know they must reach certain benchmarks within a certain time frame in order to meet their goals: eating certain foods and avoiding others, running a certain distance a certain number of days a week. These decisions adhere to their master plan. Consequently, daily decisions become easier for them and, eventually, become second nature.

Motivated people run every day of their lives, regardless

of the weather. They have already made the decision to do so long before any rain falls, so all subsequent decisions related to that goal are easy. At the top of their to-do list every day is the notation: "I will run every day. No matter what."

To Do: "Decide when and where to run, then go do it."

It is simple. Once you have clearly pictured what you want to achieve, deciding how to do it will come much more easily. After all, a plan is just a series of clearly defined decisions executed one after the other.

For several years, our town hosted a golf tournament called The Eisenhower. Many professional golfers came, and it was an exciting time to meet them and socialize with everyone at the event. One year, I was standing near one of the greens with my wife and suddenly said to her, "Next year, we'll be right in the middle of that, and I'm going to play in The Eisenhower."

Up to that point, I had rarely, almost never, played golf. Still, I saw myself out there on the greens the following year. I just had no idea at that moment how I was going to do it.

However, because I had a clear vision of what I wanted to do, my decisions about how to do it came easily. It was simply a matter of seeing my goal, coming up with a plan to achieve it, and following it through.

The first decision I made was to sign up for golf lessons the very next week so I wouldn't kill anybody! (I had always wanted to learn how to play golf, but people always said it would be a lot more fun if I could actually find my ball.) Before my first lesson, I had to decide what kind of shoes to buy, what clubs to use, and what clothing I would need for the course. I took baby steps toward that goal, and a year later I reached a 13 handicap and played in the Eisenhower. Much to my family's surprise, I stuck with it, and I'm right at a 10 handicap today.

Once people understand the power of discovering what is most important to them and creating a step-by-step plan to achieve it, things begin to fall into place. First, their energy and enthusiasm increases. Suddenly they begin reaching key destinations in their lives, spending more time with family and friends and less time working at the office, expanding their personalities into the people they envisioned they could be, and deepening their relationships with others.

They develop a heightened sense of their own personal values and begin making important decisions based on those values, aligning themselves with other people who share the same goals. These people start creating the lives they have dreamed of living.

So, Where Do You Start?

I see another common thread in the lives of my clients

who are just beginning to put their plans into action. They want to do it all by themselves right now, which is the opposite of what needs to happen.

Most people realize that following a plan of action means creating an order in which to accomplish their goals. The newer clients know that there are things they must do, but they don't realize that there are also things they must stop doing, which must become a part of their plan as well. Some activities have to be reduced or eliminated, and some have to be delegated in order for them to be free to pursue what is most important. It's also important to learn when they need to do things themselves and when to team up with others.

Winning By A Nose

"Success is not final, failure is not fatal: It is the courage to continue that counts."
- Winston Churchill

S uccess is most often a "win by a nose." The phrase originated sometime in the mid-1800s to describe a horse race that was so close that only the nose of the winning horse came in ahead of another horse. The difference in prize money between the top two winning horses was staggering. However, the win itself was only by a small margin. In racing, one horse just has to be a little bit faster and better conditioned, and that extra little bit makes all the difference.

An image of a marathon sprang to mind. I am not a long-distance runner by any means, nor am I necessarily interested in becoming one anytime soon. However, a few weeks before, I had experienced a marathon through the eyes of an avid runner. One of my co-workers had invited our family to watch his wife run the White Rock Lake marathon near Dallas. As my brother and I waited at the finish line, along with several hundred other faithful friends and family members of the runners, I was amazed by what I saw. The excitement was palpable, as each exhausted runner crossed the finish line. Some panted, their hands on their hips as they slowed to a walking pace, while others slowed and fell into the arms of their waiting loved ones, who them and cheered.

The Santa Anita Handicap in California, considered one of the most important wintertime races for thoroughbreds in North America, carries a top purse of one million dollars. In the 1930s, a horse by the name of Seabiscuit captured the nation's attention as "the little horse that could" because he raced and won against horses twice his size.

However, Seabiscuit had never won the famed Santa Anita Handicap. In fact, he had suffered two frustrating losses in 1937 and 1938 during what proved to be extremely close races. Not long after his second defeat, Seabiscuit retired from horse racing due to injuries. Nevertheless, the idea of winning the Santa Anita lingered.

In 1940, too stubborn to quit, Seabiscuit's team, led by his owner Charles S. Howard and trainer Tom Smith, made secret plans to enter Seabiscuit in the Santa Anita Handicap. This race was one of the most prestigious and richest horse races in the United States at the time.

Seabiscuit had been dealing with injuries and setbacks, but his team decided to enter him in the race despite the doubts of many. They kept their plans hidden to avoid placing unnecessary pressure on the horse and to prevent other competitors from preparing specifically for

Seabiscuit winning the Santa Anita Handicap in 1940

Seabiscuit's participation.

Success is Winning By A Nose

Seabiscuit's entry into the 1940 Santa Anita Handicap generated a lot of excitement and anticipation. His jockey, Red Pollard, rode him to victory in a thrilling race, defeating the heavily favored horse, Kayak II, in a photo finish. Seabiscuit's victory in the Santa Anita Handicap is considered one of the most memorable moments in his racing career and further solidified his status as a legendary racehorse.

Losing by a nose - not once, but twice - could have been a debilitating experience for Seabiscuit, his rider, and his owner. Some thought they were wise to call it quits. However, it had quite the opposite effect on the team and actually motivated them to dig deep and secure a victory.

In life, we can miss success by such a narrow margin that, if we had just pushed ourselves a little harder or thought through our strategy a little better, it would have resulted in a different outcome altogether. Like Seabiscuit, we can either allow adversity or disappointment to cripple us or inspire us to achieve even greater things.

On his first visit to Harrow, his former school grounds, in the fall of 1941, Winston Churchill delivered one of his most notable addresses to the students. With characteristic determination he told them, "This is the lesson: never give in, never give in, never, never, never, never - in nothing, great or small, large or petty...never yield to force; never yield to the apparently overwhelming might of the enemy."

Some people are so close to being, doing, and having all that they can imagine, but they are either not willing or not able to put forth that little extra something and go all the way. So, they give in and let life's circumstances continue to beat them by a nose. Don't walk away when you could stay in for one more round. Sometimes it is just a matter of doing one thing more or one thing differently.

I remember a key employee who left my company in its infancy many years ago. I had started my company operating out of my apartment when I was a college student. He said that he was leaving because he thought another company would provide a better opportunity for growth. Those words really hurt me because we were growing at an incredible rate. I didn't believe that any other company could provide a better opportunity for growth than what we were doing.

Once he had left, I realized that I could either mope around or try to figure out what it was that this guy saw in some other company that he didn't see in us, or I could use this deep disappointment as motivation for my own growth.

I immediately went out and earned several key financial consultant designations (*CFP, CHFC, etc.*). What should have taken me years to study and achieve took only eight months - I was that focused.

When I think about my life and the lives of other successful people, I realize that success is often just winning by a nose. It is that extra something - energy, time, discipline, or focus - that someone is willing to put in that turns the tide and transforms the outcome.

Growing in the Direction of Your Dreams

I believe that many people want to go to another level - but not everyone seizes the opportunity to reach their peak performance. Unfortunately, most of us settle into a comfort zone where we rarely challenge ourselves. We stop asking the questions we need to ask, to allow us to advance to another level.

The most successful areas of our lives often just need a small tweak to become remarkable. Like polishing dull silver to a brilliant luster, ordinary families can outshine the status quo and become extraordinary if they are willing to invest a little more awareness where it counts. A plateaued business can become a high-performance business. Ordinary teams can become exemplary ones. By optimizing our strengths, we can take many areas of our lives to the next level.

George Washington Carver saw potential the size of a peanut and transformed an entire industry. An agricultural chemist and brilliant inventor, he made it his mission to find over 300 uses for the peanut, ranging from shave cream to synthetic rubber. His inventions revolutionized the economics of farming in the late 1800s, guaranteeing that the world would never see the peanut in the same way again. "When you do the common things in life in an uncommon way, you will command the attention of the world," he once said of his discoveries. If Carver could do so much with so little, just think what peanut-sized potential lies within you if you dare to discover it.

If you never challenge yourself, you will never reach your full potential. As a young man in high school, I remember telling my mom that one day I would have a certain house, a certain car, and a certain lifestyle that could make these things a reality. My mom loved me, but she did not want me to set myself up for disappointment. I took that to mean she didn't believe I could do it. The challenge she set before me was a huge motivating factor for me to decide that I would do whatever it took to do what I had envisioned as a senior in high school. Whatever you consider success to be - being a great wife, a great father, or a great businessperson - when you challenge yourself to follow that plan, I think the outcome will take care of itself.

John F. Kennedy often quoted the ancient Greek definition of happiness: *"The full utilization of your capabilities in pursuit of excellence."* Applying every measure of your strength, talent, focus, and energy toward excellence in the areas that are most important to you will bring you happiness and fulfillment like you have never known.

What amazes me is the amount of time we have at our disposal to improve in any area of our lives. We can use our commute to and from the office or carpool to listen to an audiobook. We can call our mentor with any life questions we may have during our journey. We can read a book in the evenings. If you are consistently learning, you are progressing towards your goals.

Starting out as an independent agent, I was eager to learn all I could. I began reading motivational books and anything that taught me the art of being. Soon, I had found a mentor and encountered several peers with similar ambitions. We talked about our objectives and continually encouraged one another. I invested in the experience of those who had gone before me. I was already focused on achieving peak performance in every aspect of my life, and now I had people aiding me.

Did it take extra time out of my day? Yes. Did it require additional effort and energy? Certainly. We rarely feel the thrill of dreaming a little bigger, applying extra energy towards a greater goal and winning by a nose unless we sacrifice. However, when we step outside of the box to tackle something difficult and have the courage to believe that we can do it, we begin building momentum. I cannot think of anything more frustrating than missing out on the life we always wanted to live by a nose.

It's All In The Approach

It is crucial that we continually improve our lives. How we do it will make or break our ability to improve and reach our fullest potential. Improving does not mean focusing on what is wrong and fixing it; in fact, the opposite works best. Possibility-thinkers start by focusing on what is right in their lives, businesses, homes, and communities and then figure out how to improve it.

It doesn't take any special skills to point out what is wrong with someone or something else. However, it takes a passion for possibility to create a habit of identifying what is going well in a family, in a business, in a relationship, or in a community and then consistently seeking ways to improve it. Possibility-thinkers are never satisfied with the status quo. "Good enough" is the enemy of what is best in our personal lives, jobs, and relationships. "Good enough" is just arriving at a place where life doesn't hurt. "Good enough" is the stepsister of "fantastic and amazing." "Good enough" is a survivor, not a thriver. Unfortunately, these days we even hand out trophies and awards for "good enough."

In February 2008, the Seattle-based coffee giant Starbucks surprised the business world (and many of its customers) by closing close to seven thousand of its U.S. locations for a day to hold an intensive three-hour training session for its baristas. The chief executive of Starbucks said on the company website that the point of the nationwide closure was to "teach, educate, and share our love of coffee and the art of espresso" with its employees.

That is possibility thinking in action.

Was something drastically wrong with the company that they had to hold this training? No, in fact, it was just the opposite. They decided to improve on a good thing while things were going well.

This is completely contrary to our natural way of thinking. When we are ready to improve areas in our lives, what do we naturally want to do? We focus on what is wrong and try to fix it! If it is our business, we focus on the less productive employee. If it is our family, we focus on the rebellious child's habits.

Have you heard the phrase, "Love is blind?" We often hear this phrase in the context of relationships between men and women who are so in love that they look past each other's idiosyncrasies and imperfections. That is true love. Love does not concentrate on weaknesses and errors and try to fix them; it focuses on strengths and beauty.

I Love You. You're Perfect. Now Change.

Have you ever noticed how often we try to change the people we love? There was a popular Broadway play with the humorous title, "I Love You. You're Perfect. Now Change," which explored this concept. For example, a woman may fall in love with a charming guy who has an outgoing personality and many friends. She loves the way he handles a crowd and how he welcomes new people into the group as if they were long-lost friends.

Fast-forward 10 months to when the couple is standing at the altar getting married, and a few more months after that. They are spending every moment together, eating dinner at home and renting movies to watch on the weekends. He is growing restless to be with his friends, and she is hurt because she wonders why he doesn't want to spend all of his time with her.

He is happy to stay at home and read books together on the couch in order to avoid a confrontation, but that is not the guy she married. Whether she realizes it or not, she is trying to change his core personality.

Suddenly, love has its eyes wide open and is no longer blind to certain faults. If this couple in our example is not careful, their relationship will soon be headed in the wrong direction.

I have found that the principle "love is blind" applies in a much greater context within our offices, community groups, churches, schools - anywhere you find people in relationships with each other. You will use your time much more efficiently if you spend it honing someone's strengths instead of trying to fix their weaknesses.

A recent Gallup poll revealed that most unhappy employees quit because of their managers, not necessarily because they disliked their jobs or the company. As Marcus Buckingham notes in his book, "First, Break All the Rules," too many managers spend too much time trying to correct someone's weaknesses, rather than focusing on their strengths.

But what do we do with the weaknesses in the meantime? (And by weakness, I mean anything that deviates from what we expect another person to be or do.)

Overlook It

One way of dealing with a person's weakness is to overlook it altogether. Most personality assessment tests teach that every personality strength has an underlying weakness. Those we associate as strong, leader-type Lions can be abrasive, and the Beavers who like to get things done can work themselves to exhaustion. Every personality profile has its accompanying weakness. You'll find it if you look hard enough. Why go looking for weakness?

Reframe It

Another way of dealing with someone's weakness is to

reframe it. At work, the way a leader perceives a particular weakness can control its impact on the individual and their job performance. You can empower a weakness by fixating on it so much that you begin to associate the individual with the weakness. You may say, "That Sally - she's not a math person." Maybe that is true about Sally, but why not focus on her strengths instead? "That Sally-she's a genius at organizing things."

Delegate It

A third way to deal with someone's weaknesses is something we discussed in an earlier chapter: learn to delegate it. Delegate what people are not good at doing so that they are free to pursue what they are good at doing. This will do wonders for their self-esteem and save you a lot of headaches. It's unwise to continue to ask someone to focus on their weaknesses and expect a good result. All that does is reduce productivity and weaken the person involved. A better way is to delegate that task and help them discover what else they are really good at doing.

Finding Out What Someone Loves to Do

When you ask people to tell you about their passions, several things occur. Firstly, you honor them by simply being interested in who they are. Secondly, you get to witness what excites them. Thirdly, you get to share and benefit from the very best they have to offer. Showing personal interest in your employees and family encourages loyalty.

You can see this principle at work in families. Parents may mean well when they sign up a child for piano lessons;

however, what if the child really doesn't like the piano but comes to life on the basketball court? Which activity do you think will be easier to get the child to practice at home: piano or basketball? Sometimes, we make it difficult on ourselves by not listening to what lights people up.

Passion is an internal endeavor, and attempting to coerce, persuade, or stimulate someone to cultivate enthusiasm for an activity or job duty that they do not enjoy will never succeed. Utilize their innate talents and capabilities instead.

Even knowing what a person hates to do can be very revealing. I always ask potential employees, "What do you love to do and what do you hate to do? What do you want to do more of in your job and what do you want to do less of?" When people merely tolerate the things about their job that they don't enjoy doing, morale declines and productivity sinks.

By contrast, when you love what you're doing, work is play and you are naturally passionate about it. Productivity increases when we are having fun and doing what we do best. People often become mediocre in life for two reasons. Firstly, they are so busy trying to address their weaknesses that they forget to develop their strengths; or secondly, they are attempting to fit into the vision their boss/parent/partner has for their lives. People who are passionate about their work see their jobs as an opportunity to play and grow simultaneously. I believe the most miserable thing anyone could do is to take something as precious as life and live it without any enjoyment.

We all have untapped potential. Remember to constantly ask yourself, "What do I love to do?" This voyage of self-discovery may take you on some amazing adventures in your life.

I also see the principle of "love is blind" playing out in the business world in the way business leaders hire people and build job descriptions around them. A good leader recognizes the individuals behind the job titles or roles in the office. Instead of seeing five accountants, a receptionist, and an assistant in the office, a good leader does the math and sees seven individuals, with seven different strengths, all working for one team.

Job descriptions are stagnant, two-dimensional descriptions on paper. They lack depth. Individuals develop. Their job descriptions should evolve with them, enabling them to relinquish the responsibilities they have outgrown and seek out new challenges that are slightly beyond their current capabilities.

Although it is human nature to want to focus on what we do, that is not what makes us who we are. To have a team of highly motivated individuals, you must allow for independent thinking. You may think you have your team's potential all figured out, but if you focus on them as individuals, they will always surprise you by doing even more than they thought they could.

Getting the Right Player in the Correct Position

Every professional sports team uses systems in one of two ways to utilize the talents of their team. Some coaches apply the system to the talent; others apply the talent to the system. However, if you do not have a system that fits your talent, it will not work. Likewise, if you do not have the right kind of talent to fit your system, it will not work either.

I remember a time when a sales assistant and a service assistant both worked in my office. They had been recently hired, about two or three months into their roles. Although both people were capable of functioning in either role, I could see that their productivity level was not what it could be in either case. They enjoyed the work, but they weren't playing to their strengths. One day I asked them what they liked and disliked about their respective roles.

Their answers revealed their true gifts and showed me exactly what needed to happen; we flipped their jobs, with the sales assistant going into the service department and the service assistant stepping right into the sales role. We wrote job descriptions around each one's aptitudes that would add value to the company and set them free from their old responsibilities, resulting in two happy team players whose productivity soared within days of starting their new jobs.

In his book *Good to Great*, American researcher and consultant Jim Collins writes about having the right people on the "bus" (the analogy he uses for a team or company), but they're in the wrong seats. You don't want to kick them off the bus, but something needs to change. Once you get the right people into the right positions and they start to play on the team, everything begins to click and new possibilities unfold.

People Have to Want to Change

We are not in a position to optimize other people's roles in our business or at home if they do not want to change. All the roadmaps to success, goal-setting, and mentoring are useless unless the team players want to change.

Why is that? Simple. When we try to change others, they often think we are saying, in essence, *"I don't like something about who you are."*

One of the most important lessons about winning by a nose and reaching the next level in life is to realize the importance of *wanting to change.*

Success is based on what needs to be changed, not who needs to be changed. Ask yourself, *"What* about this situation needs to be changed?" In the context of someone's strengths, change is acceptable if it means to simply improve or mature an area where someone already has a natural affinity or talent and take it to the next level.

Character is the Antidote to Weakness

It is similar to performing the work of a blacksmith. A piece of steel goes through a process of change called tempering. A blacksmith builds strength on strength in a piece of steel by placing it in an intense flame, pulling it out and hammering it until it cools. This process does not eliminate weaknesses in the steel; it builds layer upon layer of strength in the metal until it is suitable for the task for which it is required.

That's what it means to develop one's character; character is not what is left over once all weaknesses have been eliminated. In fact, strengthening one's abilities ultimately allows for weaknesses to become redundant and fall away. If you try to eliminate weaknesses without focusing on strengths, all you will have at the end is a broken spirit and a defeated mindset.

Character is the culmination of the strengths built into our lives that determine our responses regardless of the situation. It develops over time, and it needs to be constantly refined. When character is developed consciously, it becomes the antidote to weakness. I have found that when I focus on honing my personal strengths, the weaknesses often take care of themselves.

Consider a child who brings home a report card to mom and dad. The report has straight A's, except for a C in chemistry. What gets the parents' attention first? Unfortunately, the temptation is to forfeit the opportunity to praise the child for the outstanding work in the other subjects in favor of pointing out the lower grade.

Try focusing on the A's and see what happens. Nurture the child's character by praising their diligence and hard work. Affirm the personal discipline and strength of character they showed in earning such good grades. Children absorb personal praise, especially from their parents, like a sponge. See if the C's start turning into B's over time and possibly even A's. The deficiency will have taken care of itself.

Cultivating Character

Have you ever noticed how much emphasis is placed on doing all the right things so that you can have the life you want? We are bombarded with new and improved ways of doing things in our jobs, relationships, and personal lives that will produce success. However, there is far too little formal training on how to become a better person. Everything starts with the building blocks inside of us called character. Sometimes, the most difficult place to start believing we can make a change is within ourselves. Encouraging ourselves to become the people we want to be will motivate us to live life on purpose and constantly pursue possibilities and opportunities.

Surrounding Yourself with People Who Motivate

"Surround yourself with people who believe in your dreams,
encourage your ideas, support your ambitions,
and bring out the best in you."
- Roy T. Bennet

I'm always thinking about tomorrow. When someone is on the Moon, I'm already thinking about Mars.

As a father, I remember my daughter wobbling down the hallway towards me when she was just learning to walk. As she took those first steps, I was already thinking about what life would be like when she was a teenager. I was so afraid it would all go by too fast. I remember saying to myself that in just ten short years this little grinning child, stutter-stepping her way down the hall towards my open arms would be saying to me, hands on hips, "Dad, you just don't understand!"

In fact, much to my wife's chagrin, when my daughter was

Jose, Wanda, and April Feliciano

small I took out a video recorder and recorded a message for her to listen to in anticipation of that day. I told her in that message that I knew the time was coming when she would be a teenager and would feel like I no longer understood her or her world. Even so, I assured her that I would always love her and be there for her.

Sure enough, the years flew by as predicted. When she was 12 years old, we had a situation where she wanted to do something and I said no. Would you believe the words that came out of her mouth? "Dad, you don't understand! Get with the times, Dad, so-and-so is doing this..." The timing was perfect. I grinned at her and asked her to wait while I went and got that 10-year-old tape. I sat her down and we watched it together. Nothing more needed to be said.

You don't have to have a teenager at home to realize that life is moving us forward at a rapid pace. Racecar driver, Mario Andretti, observed, "If everything seems to be under control, you're just not going fast enough." Some people prefer a slower pace and are content to dwell on past achievements and accomplishments. I never tire of the thrill of hugging the curves and shifting into the next gear towards the future. I like being around people who fuel your enthusiasm for your dreams.

Knowing Anything is Possible

Some people know exactly where they want to go and how to get there. Most people, however, have little idea. Few of us have been taught to dream or expect more. Many of us allow life's current to carry us along without giving much thought to where it is taking us. Ben Franklin once said of this type of attitude, "Blessed is he who expects nothing, for he shall receive it."

Many of us do not think we deserve much. Convinced that we do not deserve the dream, we invent excuses and let our dreams die a little every time we make a logical disclaimer.

Positive thinking attracts good things even during tough times. I refuse to settle for less. That is what a passion for possibilities is all about. I have learned to surround myself with people who think the same way. The people who will motivate you will have certain characteristics, starting with a clear vision.

People with a Clear Vision

Alan Kay, a pioneering computer scientist and one of the leading figures in the computer revolution, has said, "The best way to predict the future is to invent it." You should

Jose Feliciano

surround yourself with people who have a clear vision of a definite future and who are willing to work towards it - even if they have to "invent" it.

Alice learned this lesson in Alice in Wonderland when she was searching for a way out of Wonderland and came to a fork in the road. "Could you tell me, please, which way I should go from here?" she asked the wise Cheshire Cat. "That depends a good deal on where you want to get to," the cat responded. However, Alice replied that she really did not care much. The smiling cat told her, "Then it doesn't matter which way you go."

Having a clear vision of a bright future comes naturally for some people; they are progressive thinkers, insatiably curious, and obsessed with how things could be rather than how they are. Others are more comfortable living in the past and only have a clear recollection of how things "used to be." Surprisingly, the majority of us are taught to expect less.

Having a clear vision allows you to see the blue sky of a sunny future, even if it is raining today. By contrast, some peer at a bleak future from a clouded perspective; possibility-thinking scares and frustrates them. Looking for people who have the ability to communicate this vision to others in a way that makes sense and inspires will allow you to work faster and more effectively toward your common ideals.

People Who Think Positively

Another characteristic of people who will motivate you is unapologetic and continual positive thinking. I think Henry Ford was right when he observed, "Whether you think you can or you think you can't, you are usually right." Similarly, people with positive attitudes and outlooks on life can have a positive impact on a group. Their upbeat personality and optimism is infectious. You want that kind of attitude to replicate and spread throughout the group.

People Who Want More

Once you have achieved what others said was impossible, it liberates the entrapped mind that tells us that dreams are impossible. That adrenaline-pumping experience of succeeding when you were afraid you might fail makes you want to do it again; it is addictive.

Sadly, most people settle for less than their best and for less than life has to offer. Good leaders avoid people who limit themselves and gravitate towards, and surround themselves with, those who strive for more out of life.

After everyone in my office read the "2 Hour House" book, they began to police themselves more about how they approached problems and challenges. I didn't have to tell them that nothing was too hard or too difficult to overcome - they began to believe it for themselves. Over time, this evolved into knowing it. Once people are familiar with living life on a higher level, they realize that this is the only game worth playing. When possibility-thinking takes over an office or a team and they begin to do what others thought was impossible, the culture changes. It's charged with new-found excitement and enthusiasm for what's next. Walt Disney said it simply, "It's kind of fun to do the impossible."

People Who Support You

I once went with the Tyler Jaycees to a legislative seminar

in our state capital, Austin. They hosted a mock legislature where we would try to adopt and push through bills dealing with a variety of topics.

As one of the representatives, I had six bills to push through. The first bill was on term limits, and I was a little nervous, so I volunteered to go first. When I began presenting my bill, three other men on the opposite side of the floor stood up to counter my proposal. As I had learned to do in our instruction time before we got started, I yielded the floor to them. They began dissecting my bill like an Iron Chef.

Suddenly, I realized I had made a tremendous mistake in yielding the floor to them so soon; not surprisingly, my bill fell short by two votes, and it was my easiest bill of the session with five more to go!

As I sat there devastated, three more experienced representatives introduced themselves to me, the obvious newcomer. One of the larger men said, "Never give in to the opposition. What you should do before your next bill is to choose five or six people who agree with you. Gather them on the other side of the room and have them ask you softball questions and see if you can answer them successfully." (By the way, has anyone noticed that this has become the norm for politics these days?)

With my supporters firmly seated around the room, the effect was much more positive, and the next five bills sailed through with ease. Mahatma Gandhi, in his fight for the independence of India, said of the opposition, "First, they ignore you; then, they laugh at you; then, they fight you; then, you win."

Inspiring leaders always create a supportive environment

by outnumbering the opposition with their enthusiasm. When you have an idea, capitalize on other supporters' passion for the concept as it is being introduced - don't try to do it all by yourself. You can influence an entire room with a positive attitude towards a new idea if you have gathered enough people beforehand to express their support and enthusiasm.

People Who Believe in You

When my brother Jeff was in fourth grade, he really loved his teacher. He came home with straight A's and couldn't wait to go to school each day. I hadn't seen his face light up about school that way before, so I was curious. It turned out, the teacher was tapping into Jeff's enthusiasm by communicating to him that she believed he had great potential. She motivated him, encouraged him, and gave him a lot of self-confidence as a student.

In the same way, we can increase our potential and productivity exponentially when we feel like someone believes in us. Their confidence in our ability can boost our own self-confidence and encourage us to persist through difficult times. Of course, few of us realize that our potential and productivity can increase the most when we invest in the priceless gift of believing in ourselves.

People Who Want to Grow

Surrounding yourself with highly motivated people who want to keep growing is difficult because they are rare. I actively seek out people like that. Someone who is eager to learn and grow through challenge is inspiring to everyone around them. When you are around those who thrive on personal challenge, you will no longer be content with your own status quo.

In professional bicycle racing, the best teams learn to work more effectively by practicing a strategy called "drafting." Cyclists often race in tight-knit packs to reduce drag and the amount of energy required to maintain their speed. Applying this principle in the context of groups, it is easier for like-minded individuals to accomplish great things together because of the cumulative positive effect they have on each other.

Creating Your Own Flow

Big dreams show you what is important to you in life. Conforming to popular "can't be done" opinion is like wearing a sweater several sizes too small - it does not fit right and it limits your freedom.

There will always be negative people who tell you that you cannot achieve your goals for one reason or another. Very few people still believe that anything is possible. I prefer to be around those people.

The more I align myself with others who think positively about the challenges ahead, the less resistance I encounter as I move with the positive flow of energy they create, and the faster I can progress with my dreams and goals.

People Who Are Happy

There is a popular saying, "If Momma ain't happy, ain't nobody happy." This is true in many circumstances. Everyone suffers when an unhappy person is in a position of influence. I learned this when I joined an organization fighting against lawsuit abuse in the early nineties. Our motto was, "We all pay. We all lose." This referred to lawsuits where a jury awards exorbitant amounts of money in damages to offended individuals over something trivial. What many people don't realize is that it is not an insurance company that pays the claim; it is the business or firm. We all contribute to paying the claim through increased premiums. One unhappy person's complaint has the potential to affect us all.

I have discovered that wealthy people are not necessarily happy people. Some of the most miserable people on earth have all the money in the world. Have you ever noticed how often unhappy people tend to congregate? The law of attraction exists and it works; if you live a life that exhibits happiness, you will attract other people who are happy. If you focus on negative thoughts, you will attract others with similarly negative thoughts.

People who are happy have learned to control their fears and attitudes in such a way that nothing can steal their inner joy. These are the kind of people who motivate you, even when things seem bleak.

It's Never Too Late for Your Dreams

Traditionally, we have always accepted that we can wait too long to start being, doing, and having all that we want in life, even if there is a time limit on it. You may have heard some people divide life into three time periods: the go-go years *(20s-60s)*, the slow-go years *(60s-70s)*, and the no-go years *(80+)*.

Those imaginary lines confine us and stifle our dream

potential. We tell ourselves, "Oh no, I missed that deadline! I guess I should just give up and put my dreams away." Some people will try to put you in the slow lane, or even worse, the no-go zone where life seems much more uncertain. Recently, I have started to comprehend that these restrictions may very well prevent some of the best ideas from coming to fruition.

I always say to enjoy the journey so that you don't look back and say, "I wish I had done..." Live life to its fullest now, whatever your age. Adult children often tell their parents, "Go enjoy your money and live your life." Still, most people hold back and don't live the quality of life that they really want.

In my experience, many people who are financially secure, and even have excess money, are not doing the things they really want to do in life. In the grand scheme of life, there are more important things than money. Life truly begins when you can recognize that. Albert Einstein said, "Not everything that can be counted counts, and not everything that counts can be counted."

Luxury is being able to focus on what matters. Remember those dreams you put away? Children really mean it when they say they want you to go and enjoy life. It gives them peace of mind when they know you are having a great time.

We could all benefit from re-learning to think like a child and living for the moment. The past is the past, and the best we can do with it is to learn from it and then leave it respectfully where it belongs. We have a choice regarding what we want to do from this day forward. Life is about living in the moment and consciously making choices that will affect our future for the better.

Your Passion for Possibility

A few days after I gave my marathon speech about *Your 26 Miles* to the graduating finance class, I received a note in the mail from one of the students. At the end of my speech, I had recommended three books for those who wanted to learn more about pursuing goals and getting more out of life.

This student said he had already read all three books and asked me if there was anything else he could read in a similar vein. With graduation around the corner, most students were taking a break from books and selling them back to the campus bookstore as quickly as they could. However, this student had a passion for possibility; it takes a highly motivated person to do what he did.

As I folded the note into my desk drawer, I thought, "That's the kind of person I like to surround myself with." I called the university, found his number, and talked to him about his future plans. Within the next month, this new graduate had become a valuable member of our firm's team.

I'm still amazed at all the puzzle pieces that clicked together to get me to where I am today. When I graduated from high school and threw my hat up into the air, I had little idea what I was going to do with the rest of my life. As that hat hit the ground, my main thought was that I was done with high school forever. I knew I was going to go to college, but I did not know what major I would choose or exactly what I wanted to study.

Nevertheless, I reveled in the fact that a world of possibilities lay open before me. I felt sure that I could be anything

I wanted to be, do whatever I dreamed of doing, and have anything that hard work and desire could bring.

Then reality hit.

My first job after graduating was flagging for a road construction company for 13 hours a day in the Texas heat, earning $4 an hour. This was not my dream job. With the sun beating down on my brow and beads of sweat stinging my eyes, it didn't take long for the value of continuing my education to sink in. I realized that the hot Texas sun was sapping my dreams, and my world of possibilities was shrinking. That's when I started setting goals. My first goal was to save enough money over the summer to be able to have my own apartment, buy some used furniture and begin classes at the local junior college in the fall.

Thirty-five years later, I am more aware than ever that life is a marathon. I may have grown up since my high school days, but I still have the fiery belief inside that the whole world is open to me. I have achieved many of my life's goals so far, but in some ways I feel like I've barely begun!

Marathon runners will tell you that running is a way of life. Similarly, winning is a habit. There is always another race to run; while you are chasing one dream, the next one is lining up. A competitive marathon runner may run several races in a year; while they are training for the Boston Marathon, they may already have their eye on the New York Marathon.

Running a marathon is not an end in itself; it is merely one goal that leads to another. In your lifetime, you will likely run several marathons depending on the goals that you set for yourself. As soon as you complete one, you should have another one in your sights.

Truly lucky people live their lives purposefully and are passionate about possibilities. They never stop growing, stretching, and reaching. They have goals for their job, marriage, children, finances, retirement, community service, personal growth, and even their golf handicap!

When you're ready to face what's next on your list, be prepared to encounter a whole new set of possibilities and options. Change may be uncomfortable, intimidating, and even downright scary. Don't be surprised if the wind picks up and you have to quicken your pace. Remember this: you are entering the race that you were born to run.

"JUST BE"